I saw the cherubim one summer's night
Reaping it seemed a field of endless wheat.
I heard their voices through the fading light
Wild, strange and yet intolerably sweet.
The hour such beauty first was born on earth
The dawn of judgement had that hour begun
For some would not endure love's second birth
Preferring their own darkness to that sun.
And still love's sun must rise upon our night
For nothing can be hidden from its heat;
And in that summer evening's fading light
I saw his angels gather in the wheat:
Like beaten gold their beauty smote the air
And tongues of flame were streaming in their hair.

Fire Sonnets, 'II'

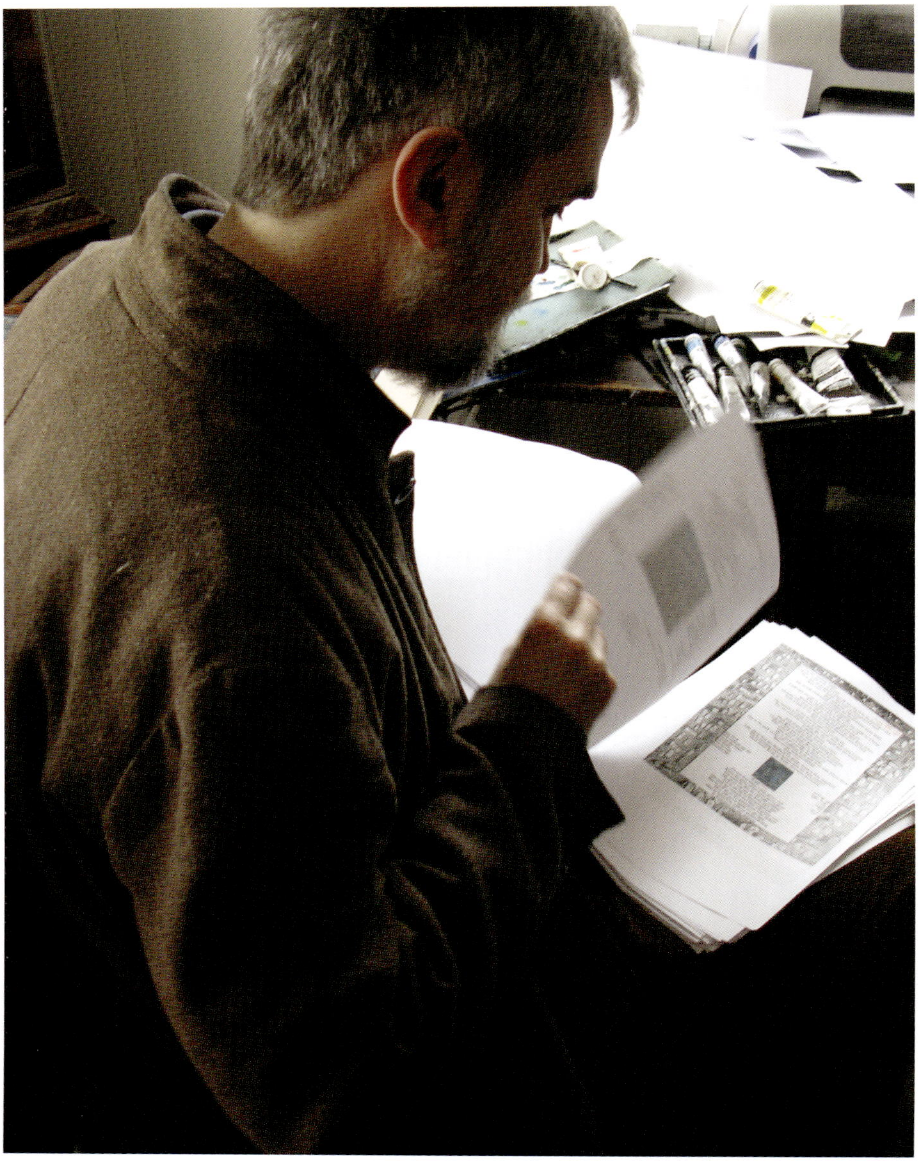

Roger Wagner
Photograph by Rupert Martin (2008)

Forms of Transcendence

The Art of Roger Wagner

Chris Miller
With a foreword by Richard Harries

PIQUANT
editions

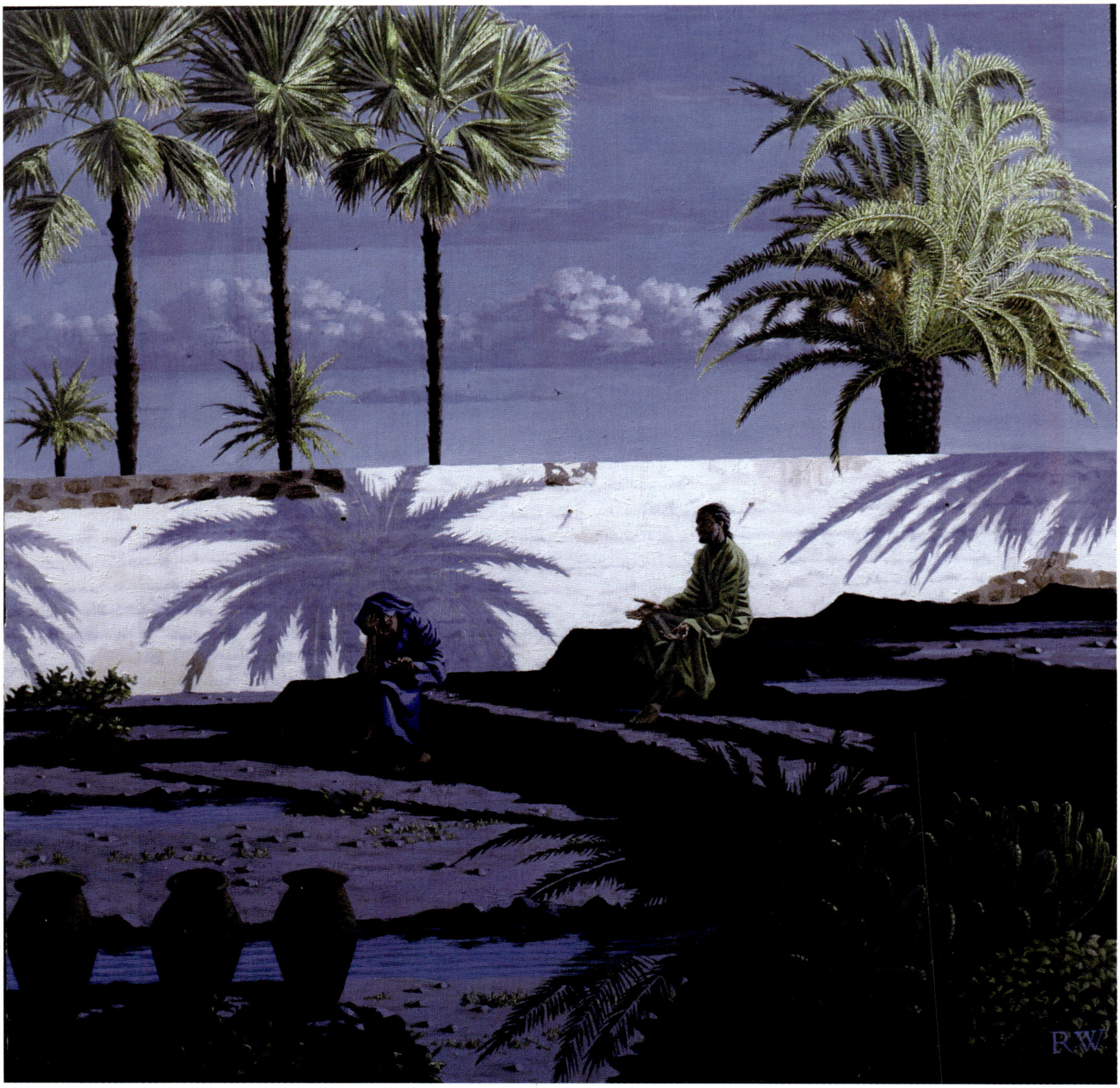

Woman Why Do You Weep? (2007)

Foreword

I have long admired Roger Wagner's work and I am delighted to see these reproductions of some of his works, accompanied by Chris Miller's helpful text.

Those whose artistic sensibility has been shaped by fashionable contemporary art receive a jolt when they first encounter Roger's work. These very direct biblical images confront what we have come to expect not only from secular art, but also from Christian art. For much contemporary Christian art has sought to avoid any impression of literalism by recourse to the abstract or semi-representational. Roger has not taken this path. Another aspect of the jolt we receive is that he has sometimes chosen biblical images which stand in sharp relief to the *zeitgeist* of our age. Take the image of harvest, for example, in his best known painting, *The Harvest Is the End of the World and the Reapers are Angels* [p17]. Not only is the image of harvest unfamiliar to city dwellers, which means most of us, but it has also been associated with the theme of judgement and comes across as threatening. But Roger's picture reshapes the way we think of judgement. This ripe, golden wheat is an image of goodness, fulfilment and flourishing. It fits in with other parables of Jesus about the seed that takes root multiplying a hundredfold and the tiniest mustard seed becoming a great tree in which the birds of the air may roost.

The obvious reason why Roger succeeds so well with images that sharply question our artistic assumptions is his consummate skill as an artist. His sheer talent forces us to think again. But no less important, of course, is the fact that there is a great deal more in the paintings than a simple attempt to reproduce what is imagined as the past. Through his use of light, choice of colours and juxtaposition of biblical and contemporary images, there is a mysterious something other present. Sometimes, too, he will take an unusual aspect of a familiar theme. So instead of the brilliantly done, much repeated, '*Noli me tangere*' from John 20, he has chosen to paint *Woman Why Do You Weep?*. But here again the shadows, light, colours and gestures hint at something more than straightforward human sympathy. Then there is the painting below [p7], where we are faced with a strikingly empty road to Emmaus, before the eye searches out a tiny group having a meal together on the roof of one of the houses.

Roger is acutely aware of the difficulties facing an artist like himself. As he has written, 'Artists who set themselves to produce contemporary religious works face formidable obstacles. To begin with there is the problem of style. The problem of how to avoid mere pastiche of what has gone before.' He goes on to mention the problem of finding a language, at a time when there is an overwhelming plurality of languages, without it simply being a private voice. Then, even more formidable, is the difficulty of finding a forum. 'In an art world where novelty and shock value are highly prized, work expressive of any kind of traditional religious commitment is unlikely to find a ready welcome. It is difficult, for instance, to imagine a conventionally religious work winning the Turner Prize.[1]

---

[1] Roger Wagner, 'Art and Faith', in *Public Life and the Place of the Church*, ed. Michael Brierley (Ashgate, 2006)

Roger has faced those difficulties and emerged with his own distinctive approach. I believe that what he has achieved at such a difficult time for an artist with a serious Christian faith will be increasingly appreciated. The fact is that nothing in life is value free: every work of art is a deeply felt response to life seen in a particular way, whether it is what Francis Bacon called his 'exhilarated despair' or Roger's deeply grounded hope.

Another major difficulty facing Christian artists today—whether musician, poet, novelist, sculptor or painter—is how to be truthful to the terrible anguish of the world, so apparent in the terrible 20th century, and at the same time express a faith that behind human life is a wise and good power. Not only are we acutely conscious of daily cruelty and torment, but we are also highly suspicious of any attempt to suggest that redemption might be possible. As Iris Murdoch put it, 'All that consoles is fake.'[2] We can question that assumption, and it is only an assumption, without in any way diminishing the problem of how we can convey a hopeful view of existence without it being dismissed as wishful thinking. Most Christian writers and artists today therefore tend to stress the suffering of life and only hint at any possibility of an ultimately redemptive outcome. But Roger's painting has what Chris Miller terms a 'serenity'. Then, in an important phrase, he points out that the beauty we see in his works is an 'aching beauty'. In short, it looks forward to what, in faith, will be—without in any way denying present reality with all its mixture of beauty and bleakness. In this respect Roger is closer to Mozart, who never conveyed the negative without the positive, than he is, say, to Mahler, for whom the balance is the other way round and who as a result has been so popular in recent decades.

George Herbert wrote of 'Heaven in ordinary'.[3] That is true of Roger's work in a number of senses. His figures are, quite deliberately, ordinary human figures. The eternal Son of God became accessible as an actual individual, Jesus of Nazareth. In one picture Roger himself and his wife appear. Stanley Spencer gave birth to his vision of heaven in ordinary things in the village of Cookham, but for him heaven was always this life seen with the eyes of love and resurrected into love. For Roger there is also 'the mysterious other'. So, for example, his painting of Jesus walking on water set before Battersea power station brings to mind Francis Thompson's poem with its reminder that

> The angels keep their ancient places;—
> Turn but a stone and start a wing!
> 'Tis ye, 'tis your estrangèd faces,
> that miss the many-splendour'd thing.

It is a poem that ends:

> And lo, Christ walking on the water,
> Not of Genesareth, but Thames!

Richard Harries (Lord Harries of Pentregarth)

[2] In her essay *The Sovereignty of Good* (Routledge & Kegan Paul, 1970)
[3] In his sonnet 'Prayer'

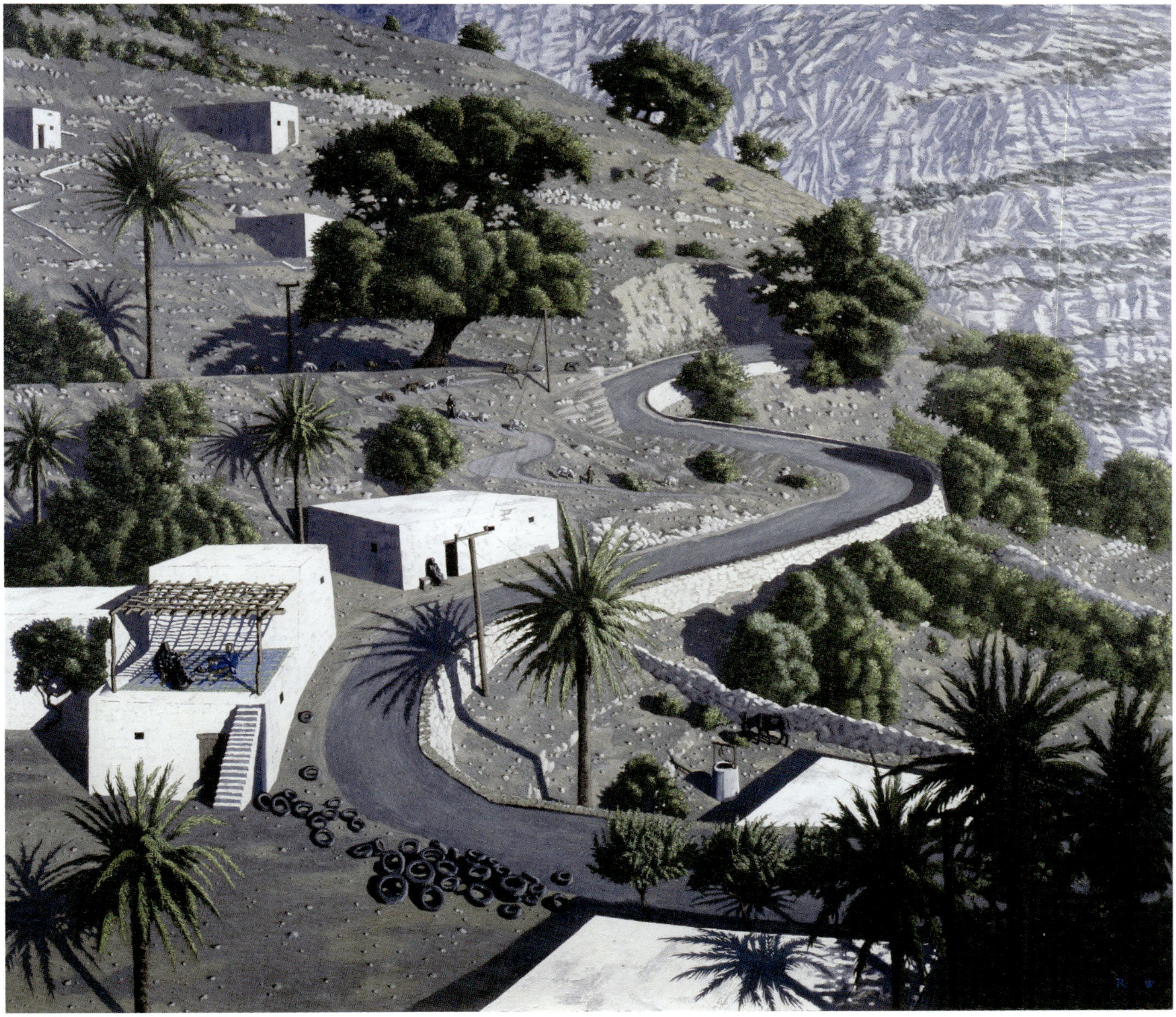

Road to Emmaus (2008)

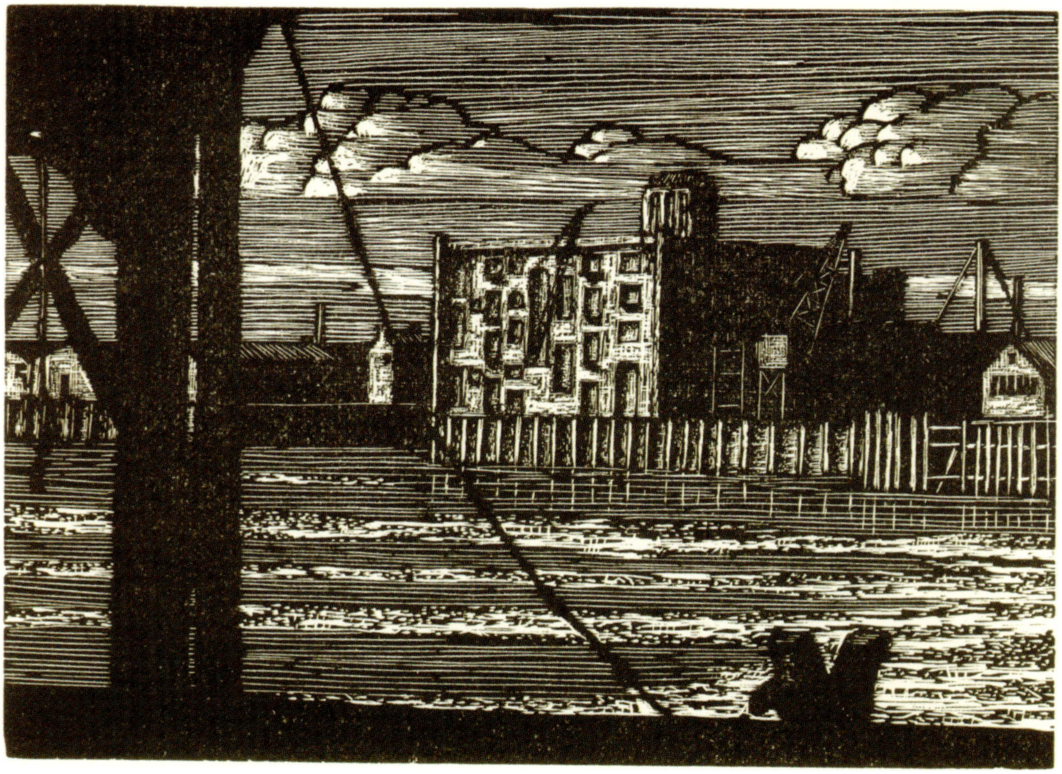

By the Waters of Babel (1988)

An Introduction
to the Art of Roger Wagner
by Chris Miller

In 1977–78, Roger Wagner was living at Mount Place in the Jericho area of Oxford in England. From there, it is a short walk along the Oxford-Birmingham canal to Port Meadow, a broad flood plain grazed by cows, its low horizons like those of a Dutch landscape painting. On the Jericho bank of the canal, a wing of Lucy's Ironworks hid from sight the magnificent copper beeches of St Sepulchre's cemetery. I remember seeing in his room at Mount Place the original of a drawing published in the Spring 1977 edition of the *Oxford Literary Journal* with an epigraph from Psalm 137: 'By the waters of Babylon/ We sat down and wept/ remembering Zion.// "Sing us" they said/ "some songs of Zion"./ How shall we sing the Lord's song/ In a strange land'. Later in the year, drawing took second place to studies—enabling Wagner to take a first-class degree.

Ten years later, Wagner published a short pamphlet, hand-printed at the Oxford Printmakers Co-operative: *In a Strange Land*.[1] It consisted of Wagner's translation of Psalm 137:1–6, printed together with the Hebrew on translucent paper, through which appeared his woodcuts of London's Docklands.[2] This pamphlet also contained two poems, 'The Mirrors' and 'Hosea's Song'. The Docklands views, framed with the stanchions of the idle cranes, showed deserted warehouses, yards graffitied by the National Front, and grass growing in tufts from the unkempt wharves. These were indeed images of desolation, but how did they relate to the captivity in Babylon?

Critics have tended—rightly—to set Wagner's work alongside that of Samuel Palmer and Stanley Spencer and, when faced with his harvesting angels, to quote Thomas Traherne, the poet of childlike innocence. It may come as a surprise, then, that the two poems in *In a Strange Land* are both about prostitution. 'The Mirrors' takes its starting point from Genesis—'So God created man in his own image'—only to focus on the degradation of that image:

> The mirrors of Almighty God
> Have Oxford Street as their love bower
> They leave their names in public phones
> And sell themselves for half an hour.

---

[1] Roger Wagner, *In a Strange Land* (Oxford: The Besalel Press, 1988)
[2] For example, *By the Waters of Babel* (1988)

In its turn, 'Hosea's Song' speaks of God paying the bride-price for an adulteress:

When he put down the going rate
And bought her back with his own life
The angel guests all kissed the bride
And welcomed her as God's own wife.

Wagner went on to execute a series of mixed media paintings of the Docklands that forms an extended accompaniment to Psalm 137. He exhibited these in 1988 at Anthony Mould's gallery in New Bond Street. They are haunting laments. Their grey, grey-blue and brown tones, layered with glazes, offer vistas of obsolescence.[3] Here are the decaying gasometers, the cranes raising their jibs like orantes, the powerful symmetry of the warehouses condemned to disuse. Forms prescribed by function had their own dignity and, as their functions leached away on the tides of commerce, the same forms came to signify their abandonment.

The Docklands, traditionally the first staging post of the migrant, were the heart of the deprived East End. With the closure of the docks in 1980, unemployment was an increasing scourge. 'Regeneration' was beginning at Canary Wharf under the aegis of Thatcherism. But Wagner is not harking back to the imperial trade for which the docks were designed nor specifically censuring the new economic conditions that had rendered the docks obsolete, for all his awareness of the suffering implicit in this transformation. That suffering has become the oppression of the captive and exiled Israelites forced to sing their songs on the shores of oppression. This in turn takes us to Hosea's metaphor of infidelity and prostitution—of the adoption of false gods in place of the true God in order to placate the new (here implicitly secular and economic) order. The history of the Jews is, for Wagner, a prophetic history, the story of the Chosen People to whom Christ would be born. Hosea's prophecy is there to assure us that God's love has, despite the Israelites' infidelity of that time, remained strong and redemptive: 'And I will sow her unto me in the earth and I will have mercy upon her that had not obtained mercy; and I will say to them which were not my people, Thou art my people; and they shall say, Thou art my God.'[4] Thus, in the metaphor of the exiled Israelites, we hear not only the prophecy of Christ's coming but also the assurance that at all times error will be forgiven. And, in the metaphor of Christ's death, we hear of a love so strong that it can overcome the degradation of the divine image and restore the soul traumatized by prostitution, glue-sniffing, racism or corruption. In the absence of activity, the decaying forms of industry convey a sense of the absence of God. Yet this is not the absence of God but the desolation of those who have turned away from him: 'If I forget you, O Jerusalem, let my right hand forget her cunning'.[5]

[3] For example, *Canning Town* (1988)
[4] Hosea 2:23
[5] Roger Wagner, *In a Strange Land* (no page numbers)

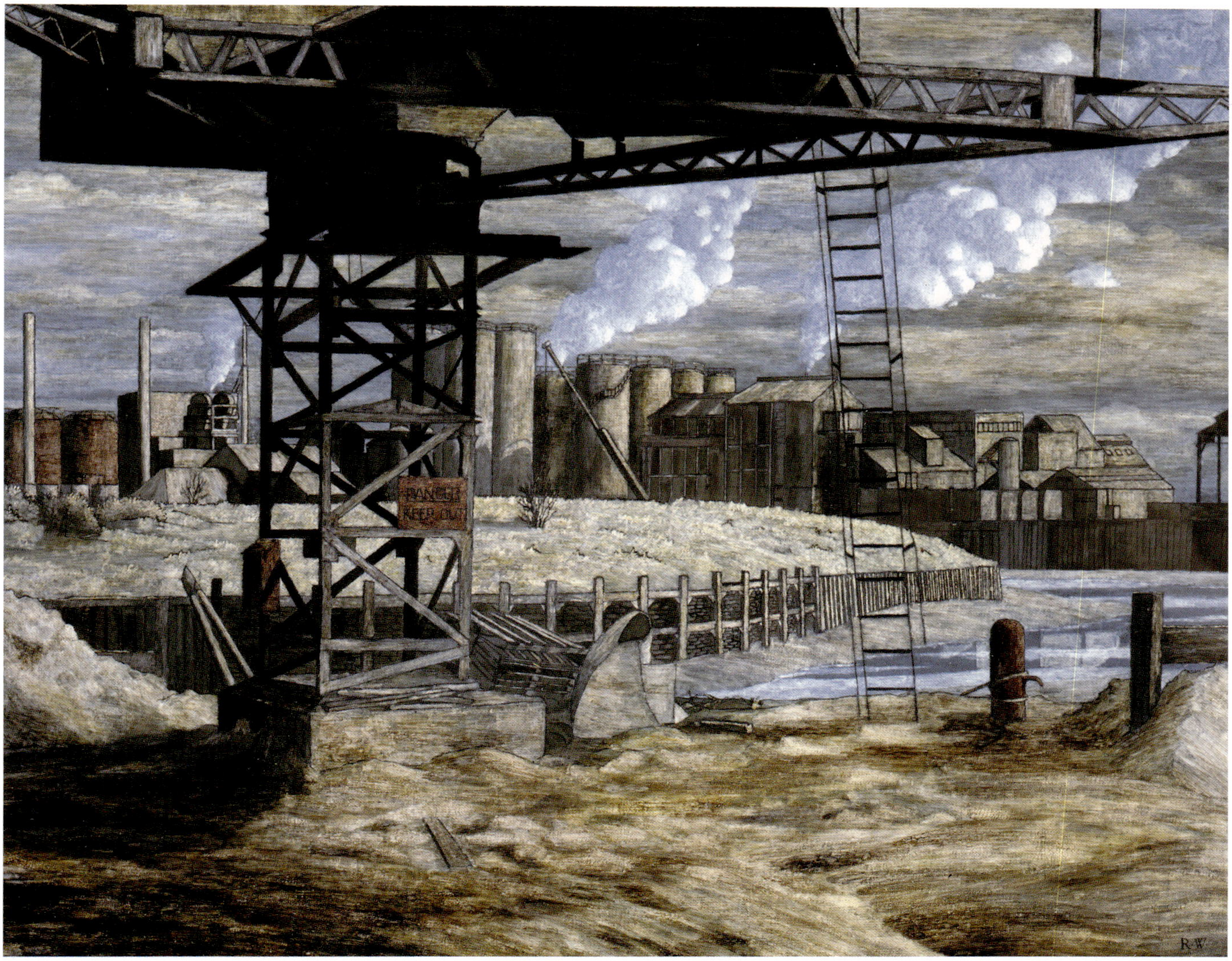

Canning Town (1988)

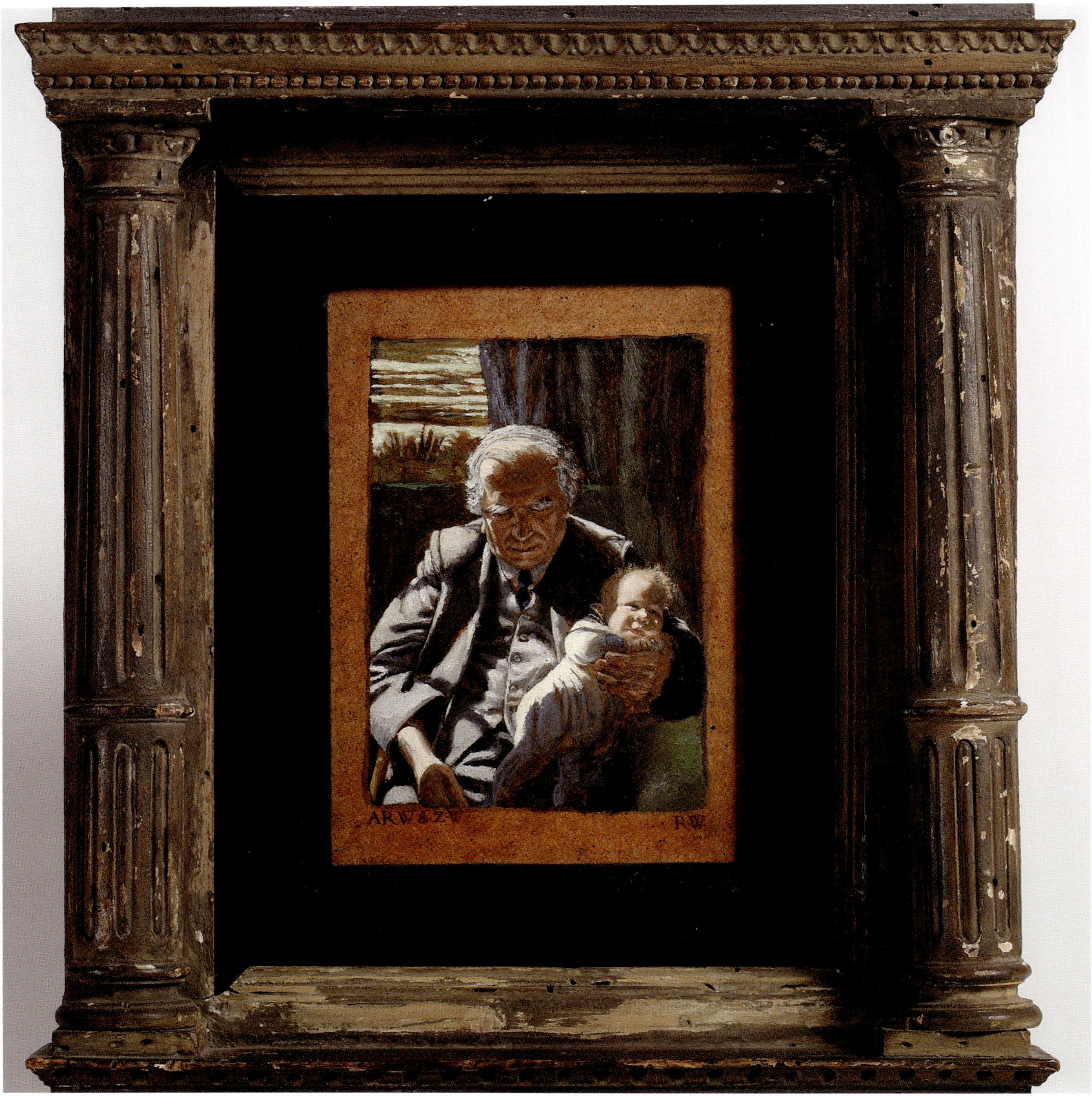

Anthony Wagner with Granddaughter (1994)

Wagner's vision is not much preoccupied with the infernal. Even when, in these poems and landscapes of the Docklands, he records the degradation of the poor and the migrant, he does so with the assurance that divine love will redeem them. Within the confines of the frame, that assurance takes the form of beauty. His work is generally the expression of faith, which I have heard him explaining to a child as trust. Acceptance and celebration are the metaphysical binding of his pigments. Consequently, the forms of his paintings tend toward serenity. To say so is not to suggest that they are confined to a kind of idyllic pastoral, to songs of innocence. On the contrary, many of the most striking images register contrasts between the modern and the biblical world. But these contrasts are only apparent. The collocation of angels and power stations asseverates the simultaneity of the biblical and modern worlds. Angels and power station co-exist and, convenient as the performance of the latter might be, the biblical stories are there to tell us that the most important spiritual events can take place without any electric light being shed at all. Spiritual and material power stand side by side but there can be no argument, even for the agnostic, about which is the more important. We live spiritual lives and suffer when we live materially comfortable lives in spiritual deprivation. We live material lives and material deprivation is suffering. But *in extremis*, physical survival itself often owes much to spiritual resource. Man does not live by bread alone.

The beauty of the Docklands paintings is an aching beauty but this nostalgia is more radical than conservatism, for the 'return' for which they ache is a Second Coming. I have turned to them first because much of Wagner's reputation has been built on his skills as a painter of metaphysical pastoral, whereas in these paintings and poems we see him treat precisely the kind of urban themes that concerned his wife, Anne, when she was working with Jackie Pullinger in the Walled City in Hong Kong to free addicts from their servitude by bringing to them a knowledge of God's love. Secondly, they illustrate the constancy of Wagner's vision and his slow, deliberate acquisition of the means by which it could be materialized. It took Wagner ten years to elaborate a symbolic code and formal mastery sufficient to illustrate Psalm 137. The result is triumphant. Entering the world of the Old Testament, the stranded lighters and rusting gantries of Bermondsey and Canning Town have acquired an almost mystical status.

On the constancy of Wagner's vision, we have the testimony of the photographer, curator and priest Rupert Martin. Theirs has been a long friendship of mutual influence. Martin notes that the subject of *The Harvest Is the End of the World and the Reapers Are Angels* first presented itself to Wagner while he was still an undergraduate.[6] It is recorded in Wagner's *Fire Sonnets*, a book of poems and engravings published in 1984[7]:

> I saw the cherubim one summer's night
> Reaping, it seemed, a field of endless wheat
> I heard their voices through the fading light
> Wild, strange and yet intolerably sweet.

During his final year at Oxford, Wagner contemplated giving up his English course to study art, in part to realize this vision. After completing his degree at Lincoln College, he did indeed go on to study at the Royal Academy, following life classes under the tuition of the Keeper of the Royal Academy Schools, his much-admired teacher Peter Greenham. After three years at the Academy, Wagner began to feel he had the technical equipment to realize his vision of angels reaping. This was a painting on a large scale and Wagner is an exceedingly slow worker, but a first completed version was nevertheless destroyed as 'too garish'.[8]

The Harvest Is the End of the World and the Reapers Are Angels was completed in 1984 and a second version in 1989 [pp17–19]. The latter has established itself as something of a classic. Alan Powers has noted: 'It is a painting without artifice, the most transparent statement of a vision that could be imagined, something everyone can understand.'[9] Martin also records Wagner's dissatisfaction with the traditional form of Last Judgement, in which the terrors of hell bulk large. This painting refers to the parable of the tares in Matthew 13:40–42: 'As therefore the tares are gathered and burned in the fire; so shall it be in the end of this world. The Son of man shall send forth his angels, and they shall gather out of his kingdom all things that offend, and them which do iniquity; And shall cast them into a furnace of fire: there shall be wailing and gnashing of teeth.'

---

[6] Rupert Martin, 'Roger Wagner's Visionary Landscapes', in *Image: A Journal of the Arts and Religion* (Summer 1995) p29. See www.rogerwagner.co.uk/articles.html

[7] 'II', in Roger Wagner, *Fire Sonnets* (Oxford: The Besalel Press, 1984), no page numbers

[8] Martin, 'Roger Wagner's Visionary Landscape', p29

[9] Alan Powers, foreword to *A Silent Voice and Other Paintings by Roger Wagner*, catalogue to the exhibition of that name at The Gallery in Cork St, London, 15–27 March 1999 (London: Anthony Mould Contemporary, 1999), no page numbers

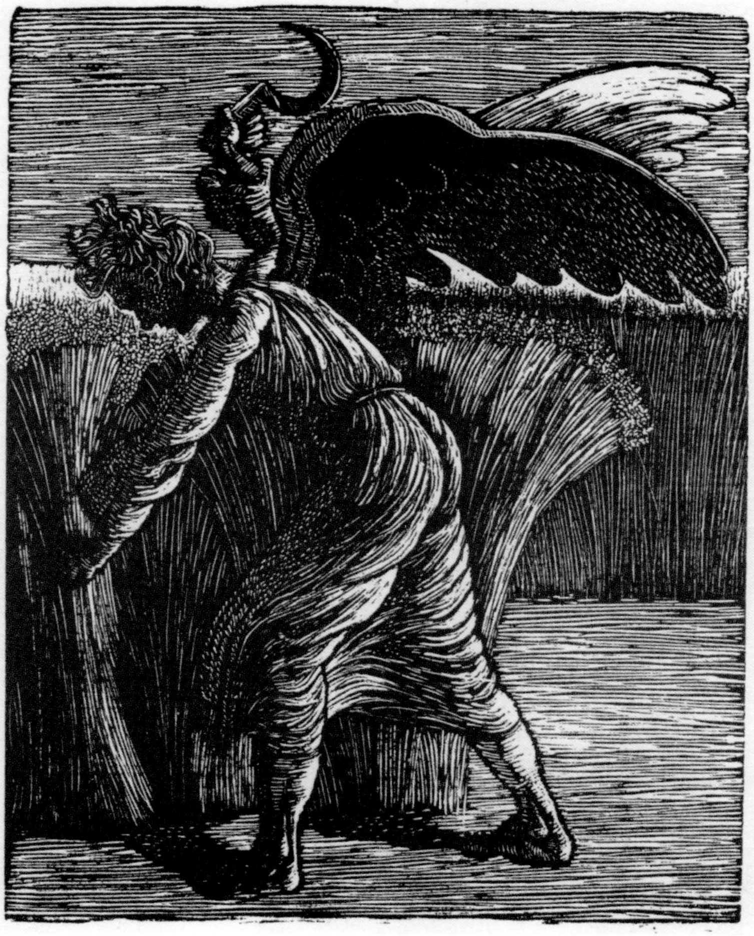

Reaping Angel (1984)

If the subject of the Last Judgement has often been represented in allegories of earthly atrocity—with devils manipulating contemporary instruments of torture such as the 'cat's paw' scrapers painted by Hans Memling in his Gdansk triptych—it is not least because the destruction of evil in human form has often been attempted by humanity, both by religious agents such as the Inquisition and secular ones such as the *Comité de salut public* of the French Revolution. To my mind, Wagner's Suffolk-world's-end vista sits ill with the redemptive vision of his Dockland paintings. Where the 'tares' are being burnt and there is 'gnashing of teeth' we might expect Christ's place to be among the 'ragged mirth'[10] of the 'tares', for whom he would willingly give his life. Wagner would quite properly say that he already has. For the secular observer, this is a disturbing vision; only the tares are cast into the flames, but the angels scythe without distinction.

The second *Harvest* is also a composition of formidable accomplishment. Though the corn is bathed in light, the shadows are long and the marsh estuary in the hinterland is already overshadowed. The sky is darkening in the east and the slant light of late afternoon is barely illuminating the thunderheads. The angels are intent on their task of scything and sheaving and will not finish their task today if human criteria are at all relevant. It is some time before the sheer conviction of Wagner's painting betrays the subtle artifices of its composition. There are two primary horizontal divisions; two further divisions are implied by the banks of corn in the foreground. And two vertical axes are marked, each a quarter of the way into the picture, by the innermost sycamore on the left and the oak on the right. The inner vertical axes, formed by the stook and scything angel (to the right) and (to the left) by the end of the foremost rank of wheat and the stooping angel's wingtip, further subdivide the composition. The St Andrew's cross laid in asymmetrical perspective across the surface of the wheat restores the eye to the primary compositional emphasis, which lies on the axis of oak and angel, while 'opening up' the perspective-space between the angels and their colleagues labouring in the distance. This Renaissance attention to geometry is less overt than, for example, in Piero della Francesca. The overdetermination of each aspect of the painting is beautifully concealed and the naturalistic predominates.

---

[10] From George Herbert's sonnet, 'Redemption': 'At length I heard a ragged noise and mirth/ Of thieves and murderers: there I him espied / Who straight, Your suit is granted, said, and died'. See George Herbert, *The Complete English Works*, ed. Ann Pasternak Slater (London: David Campell Publishers Ltd, 1995), p37.

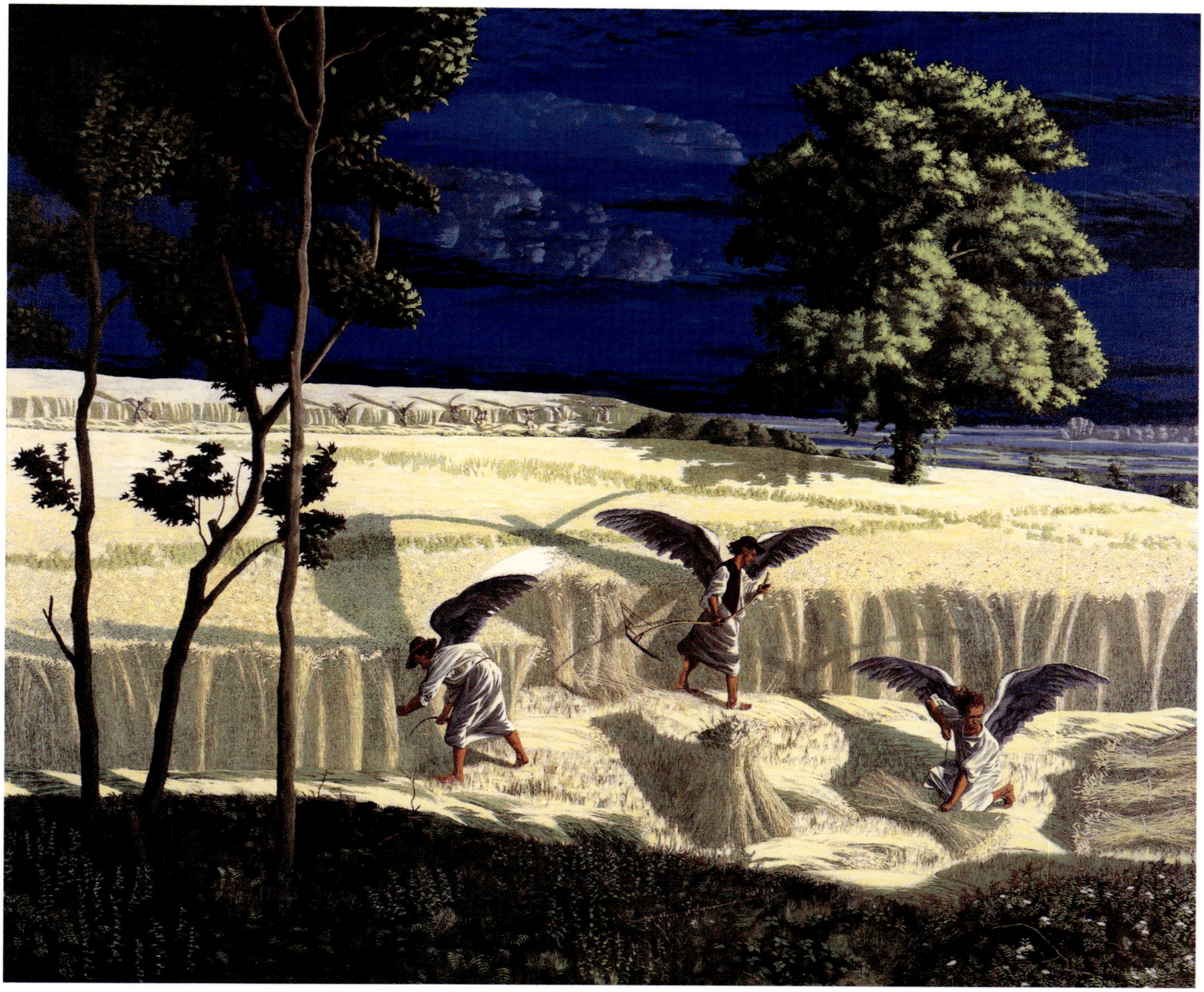

The Harvest Is the End of the World and the Reapers Are Angels (1989)

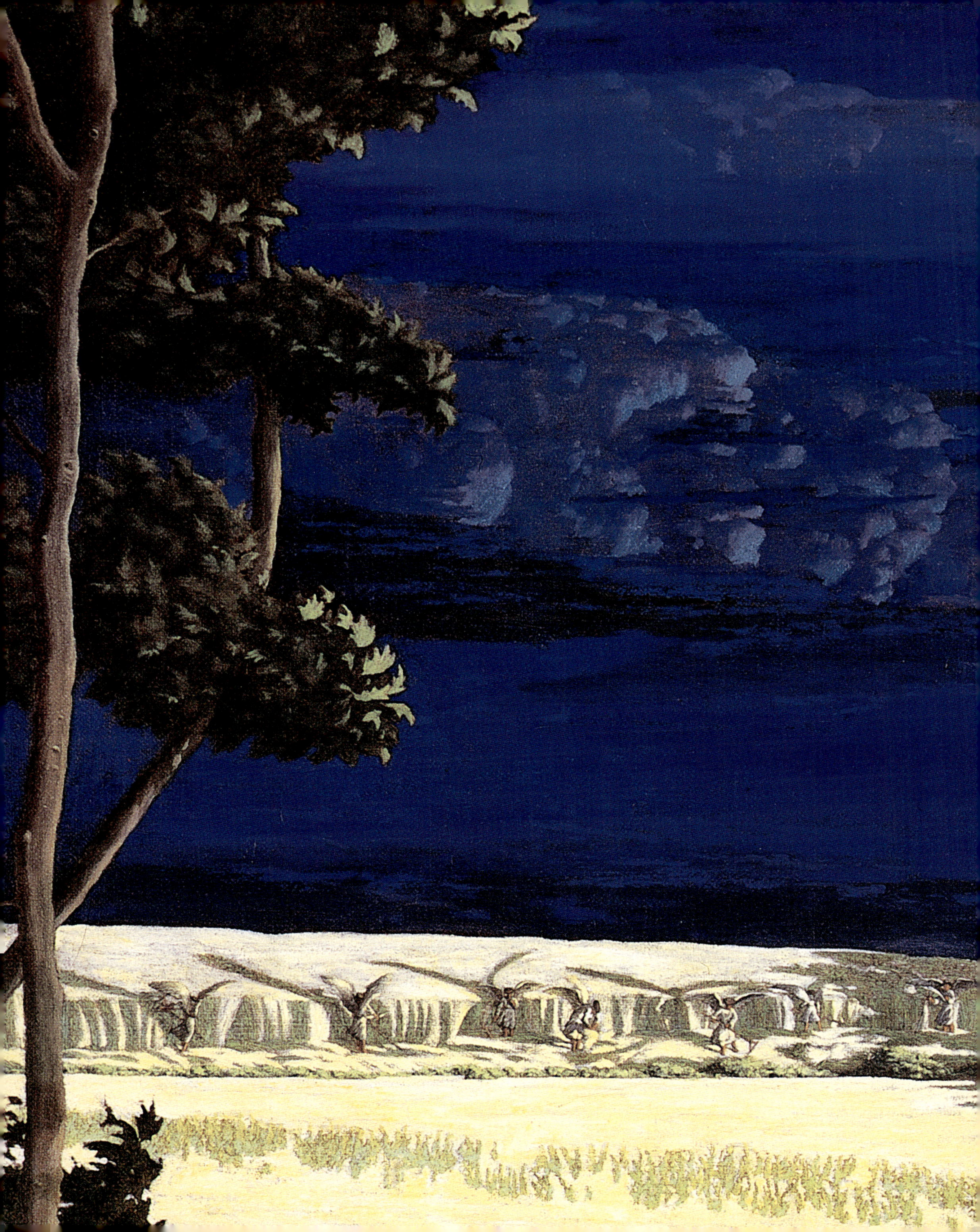

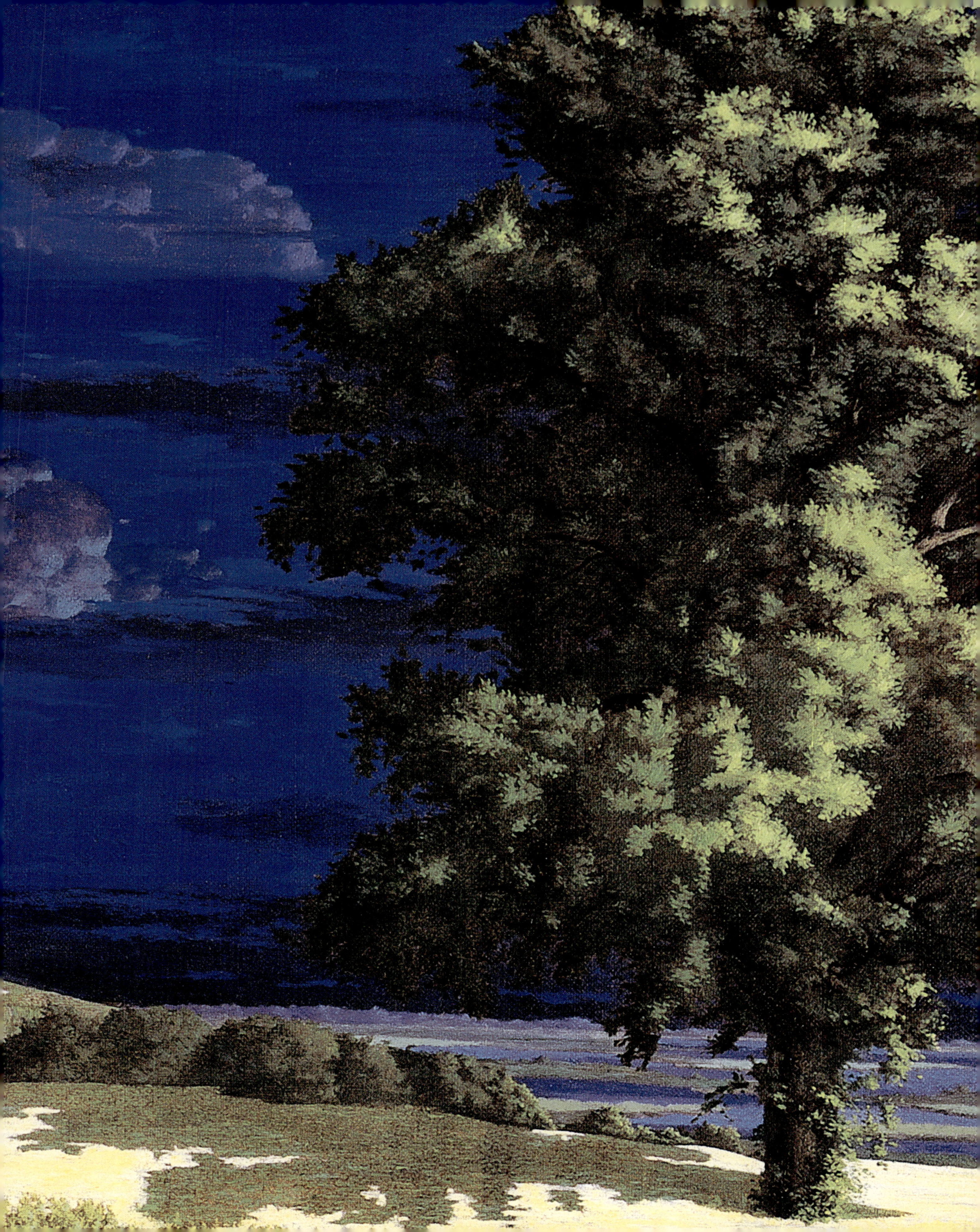

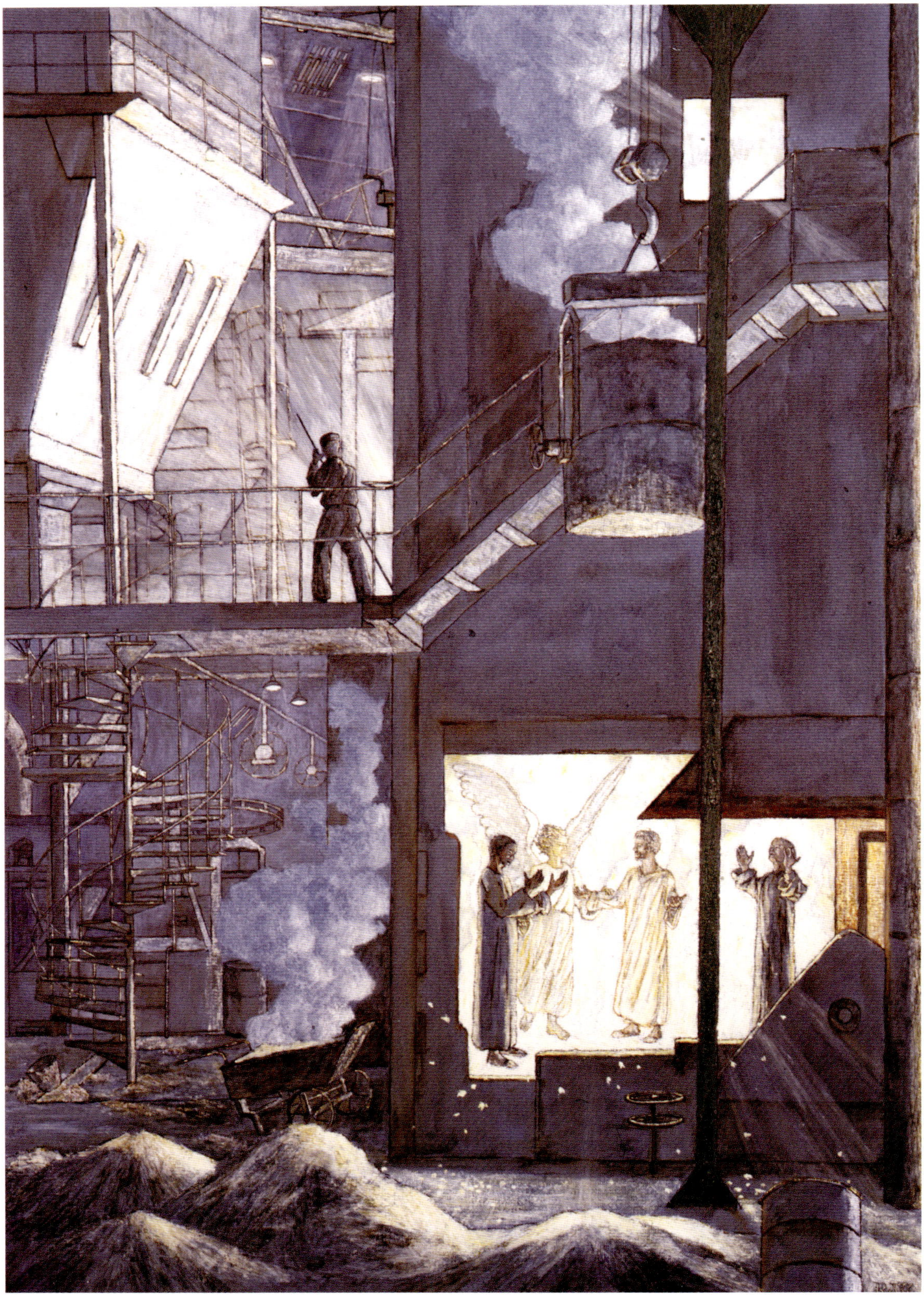

The Burning Fiery Furnace (1989)

Let me now return to Mount Place, which was then divided only by a large block of flats from Lucy's Ironworks. The factory (since demolished) was an object of fascination: its high-windowed canal-side wing was extremely narrow, so that in bright light the shadowy forms of the trees behind could be seen right through it. It surrounded St Sepulchre's cemetery on three sides, the fourth being taken by the terraced houses of Juxon Street. With the canal and railway running parallel to one of its sides, it offered a complete prospect of Victorian life. While planning his *Burning Fiery Furnace* (1989), Wagner arranged to tour the ironworks. The inside of the canal-side building proved equal to the fascination inspired by its façade: moulds cooling in a bed of sand moved on conveyor belts in the highest reaches of the building, sand drifting down from them as they blocked the light from the full-height windows. Ladders, decks and walkways gave access to the upper levels of the furnaces. The workers moved about in helmets, boots and the thick woollen jackets that protected them from molten spatter. Now and then molten metal poured out of the furnaces, the terrifying liquid surrounded by its incomparably brilliant glare.

In *Fire Sonnets,* 'VI', Wagner writes: 'And then he kissed me with a burning coal/ My sin was gone and I, at once, was free'. Here, then, in Lucy's Ironworks, was the image of God's love that he had sought. The story is that of Daniel 3, of the Jewish intendants of the province of Babylon—Shadrach, Meshach and Abednego—cast into the furnace by order of the Persian King Nebuchadnezzar because they would not honour the golden image that the king had made. Wagner's highly-structured composition gains by its asymmetry. The eye is led by the steam rising against the spiral staircase to the brilliant light against which a worker waits, steel rod in hand, to tap the furnace. From here it circles back down to the furnace itself and only then does the angel, all radiant light, emerge clearly, his two-thirds profile position echoing that of the worker, his back towards us, who stands in mirror-image to the angel, one level above. On the floor, the piles of sand act as a repoussoir, while the brightly-lit furnace chimney at the top left endlessly returns the eye to the angel.

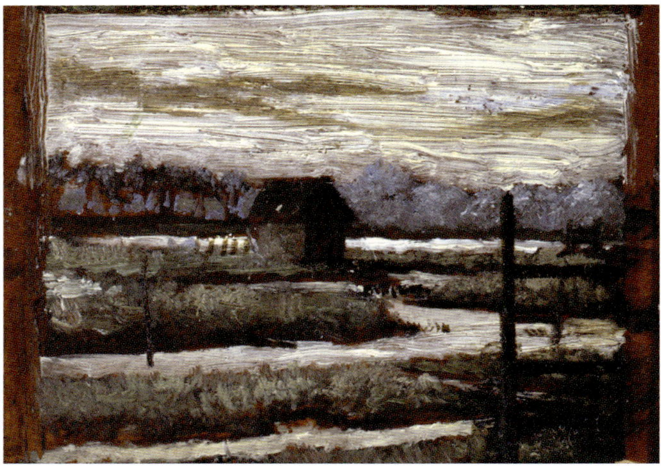

Chillesford Boathouse (1984)

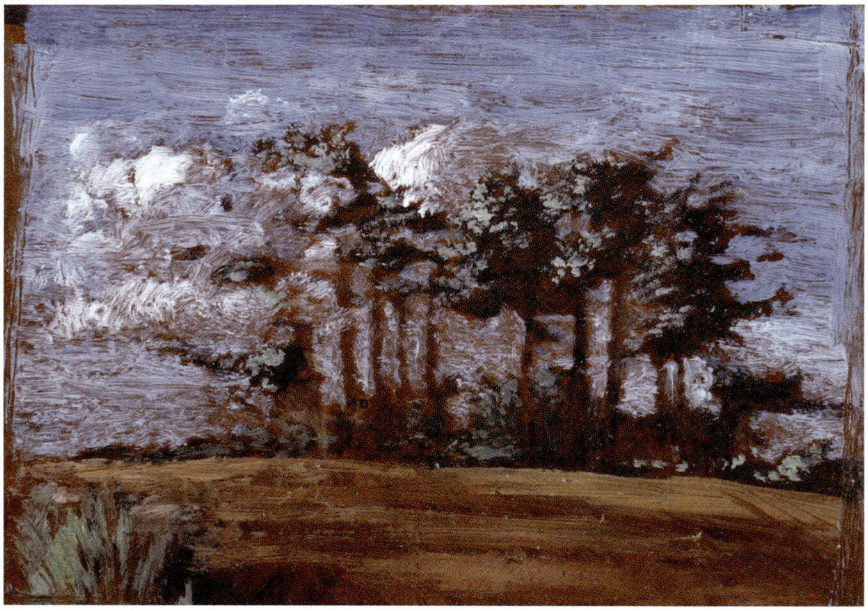

Sudbourne Trees (1984)

Burning Fiery Furnace [p20] is paradigmatic of Wagner's contention of the simultaneity of the biblical and our own epoch. Another such image is the first of Wagner's two paintings of *Abraham and the Angels* [p25]. Here the setting is one of Wagner's 'elected' landscapes. The Wagner family's holiday home was in Aldeburgh on the Suffolk coast. This is a low-lying area of agricultural land, pine forests, estuaries and long stretches of beach, and a designated Area of Outstanding Natural Beauty. For Wagner, it was the first and most important landscape of his imagination. When he thought of the biblical stories, it was here, in his childhood haunts, that he first placed them. *The Harvest* (1989) bears unmistakable traces of this in its conjunction of rich arable land with the waters of the estuary in the background. A number of early paintings, such as *Sudbourne Trees* and *Chillesford Boathouse*, both 1984, are direct records of this area. Wagner's placing of biblical scenes in a landscape familiar to his own imagination is in one sense representative of most European readings of the Middle-Eastern settings of Christ's story. Thus the Washington *Adoration* attributed to Giorgione takes place in a generic Italian landscape. The transposition to landscapes redolent of Mediterranean Europe passes almost unnoticed in Western religious painting.

But there exists a still more local tradition in English painting, one centred on Palmer and Spencer. Samuel Palmer's visionary perception of the steep chalk escarpments around the Kentish village of Shoreham was a vision as pagan as it was Christian, but there he set some religious themes, notably the *Rest on the Flight into Egypt*. Stanley Spencer's elected landscape was the little Thames-side village of Cookham, set among even steeper chalk hills that barely register in his work. He placed his *Crucifixion* and *Resurrection* specifically in the village context, while depicting other biblical scenes in more generic but clearly local settings. A very local setting such as Spencer's can, of course, seem so subjective as to lose its universality. It is one of Wagner's fortes to enrich his biblical scenes with accretions of further symbolism relating to his own times.

Wagner's *Abraham and the Angels* (1986) perfectly exemplifies this capacity. The story referred to is Genesis 18, in which 'three angels' visit Abraham at the oaks of Mamre. By featuring the nuclear power station Sizewell A, a construction perfectly uncharacteristic of his elected landscape, Wagner emphasizes not the miracle of birth to a menopausal woman but the aspect of potential destruction implicit in the story of Sodom and Gomorrah. The eruption of the serene forms of Sizewell A into the Suffolk landscape is dramatic by any standards. The scale of the power station is astonishing in itself. In Wagner's painting, the combination of nuclear generation and vast electrical output (enough for two counties) is reflected in a kind of shimmer of energy. Yet the building, for all its bulk, is nothing less than demure; it draws attention to itself with a mere puff of steam and in colour is barely distinct from the Guercino blues of the sky. The standing corn and the Scots pines and bracken of the hillock restore us to the Aldeburgh pastoral of many of Wagner's early works. But in the foreground a sinister dead bough directs us to the figures on the hillside. The angels wear cerulean robes and have cerulean wings. Abraham too is robed, though in darker, almost Marian, colours.

The serene confrontation of biblical and modern times forms an unforgettable composition. Wagner's symmetries have never been clearer. The pale and restricted palette and the sheer simplicity of the painting's organization seem at once to quieten the composition as a whole and make the presence of the nuclear reactor the more disquieting. Because we know what a nuclear accident or explosion can do, there is something ominous about the tranquillity of this painting.

If the Aldeburgh landscape is Wagner's Shoreham—his own 'spiritual landscape'—it was to the Middle East that he turned in a series of paintings born of a trip that he made in 1999 with Rupert Martin. Out of this pilgrimage came a wealth of images painted and photographic, which were shown at a combined exhibition at Eton College.[11] Although Wagner has used photography extensively in creating his patient and meticulous art, the two arts have never

[11] 'Roads to Damascus: Photographs Rupert Martin, Paintings Roger Wagner', The Brewhouse Gallery, Eton College, 17 November 2001–17 March 2002

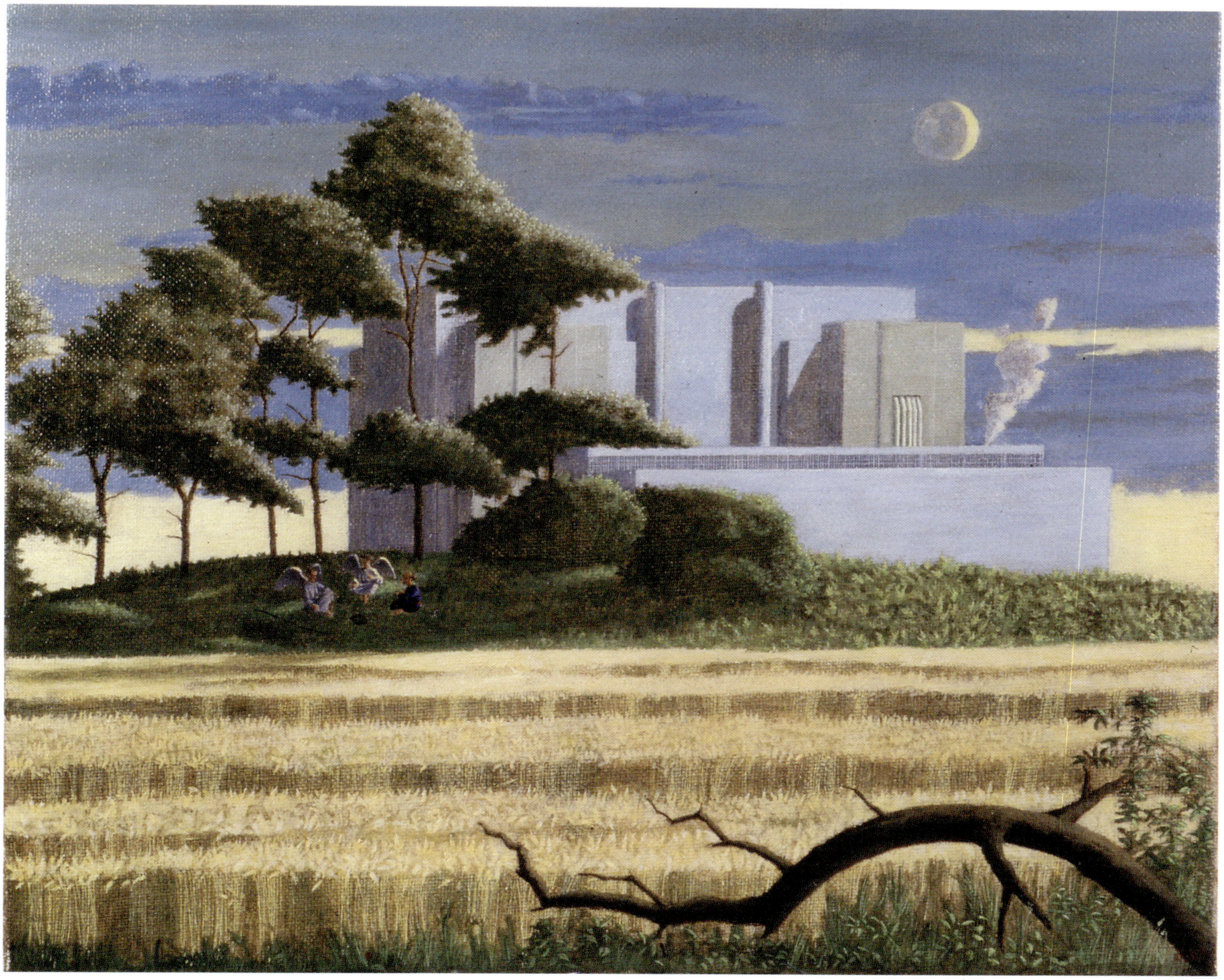

Abraham and the Angels (1986)

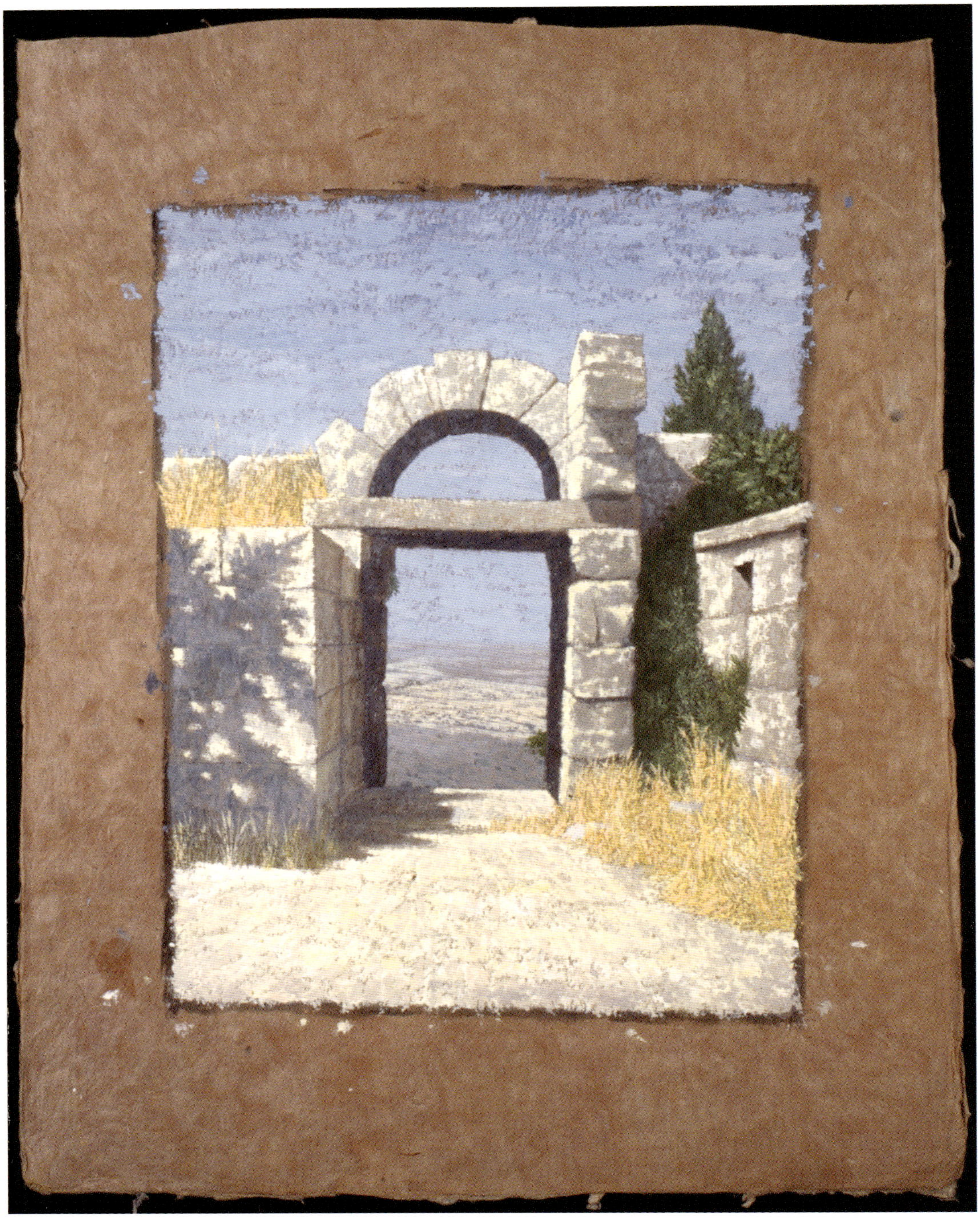

A Pilgrim Door (1998)

seemed as closely related as in his Telanissus series. Perhaps this reflects the influence of Martin's photography. The two have often travelled together, notably in Greece and Italy. At the heart of their Syrian travels was an excursion to the Qal at Simaan, the ruins of the basilica at Telanissus built by the Eastern Roman Emperor Zeno to commemorate the site where St Simeon had lived for many years atop his column. It is characteristic of Martin's photography to obtain a metaphysical effect from recording with unique acuity the vestigial remains of an order no longer present; this was true even before his conversion to the Evangelical faith. The symmetries of the extraordinary basilica on Sheik Barakat Mountain are many and satisfying. In both artists, roofless façades and unbroken arches bestride nature as plants rise like tongues of fire licking at the fallen stones. The beauty of the fragmented buildings is made to evoke a splendid order now fallen into disrepair and that faith alone can redeem.

Wagner's skies here reflect something much closer to nature than the variations of the Guercino blue that surmount his English landscapes. Through *A Pilgrim Door* (1998) we look, paradoxically, outward; the vista is no longer metaphorically but here literally towards the Promised Land. The 'high' colours of the Middle East—the silvery-gold of dried stalks, the purple-grey, roseate and yellow reflections of mica in exposed rocks and the refulgent greens of conifer and juniper—construct a new palette in these luminous paintings. Shadows have always had a structural function in Wagner's work and his compositional skills have frequently worked strong horizontal shadows into his English paintings. Now the stark contrasts and intense reflections of the Syrian light have almost to be toned down to attain the stately precision of Wagner's record of the basilica. These are paintings of place as well as faith and do not attempt to exaggerate the ruins as the Cyclopean monuments of overweening classical ancestors. But the scale and precision of Byzantine masonry is continuous with that of the Greek ruins Martin and Wagner visited together during their university years. They receive an affectionate foregrounding in

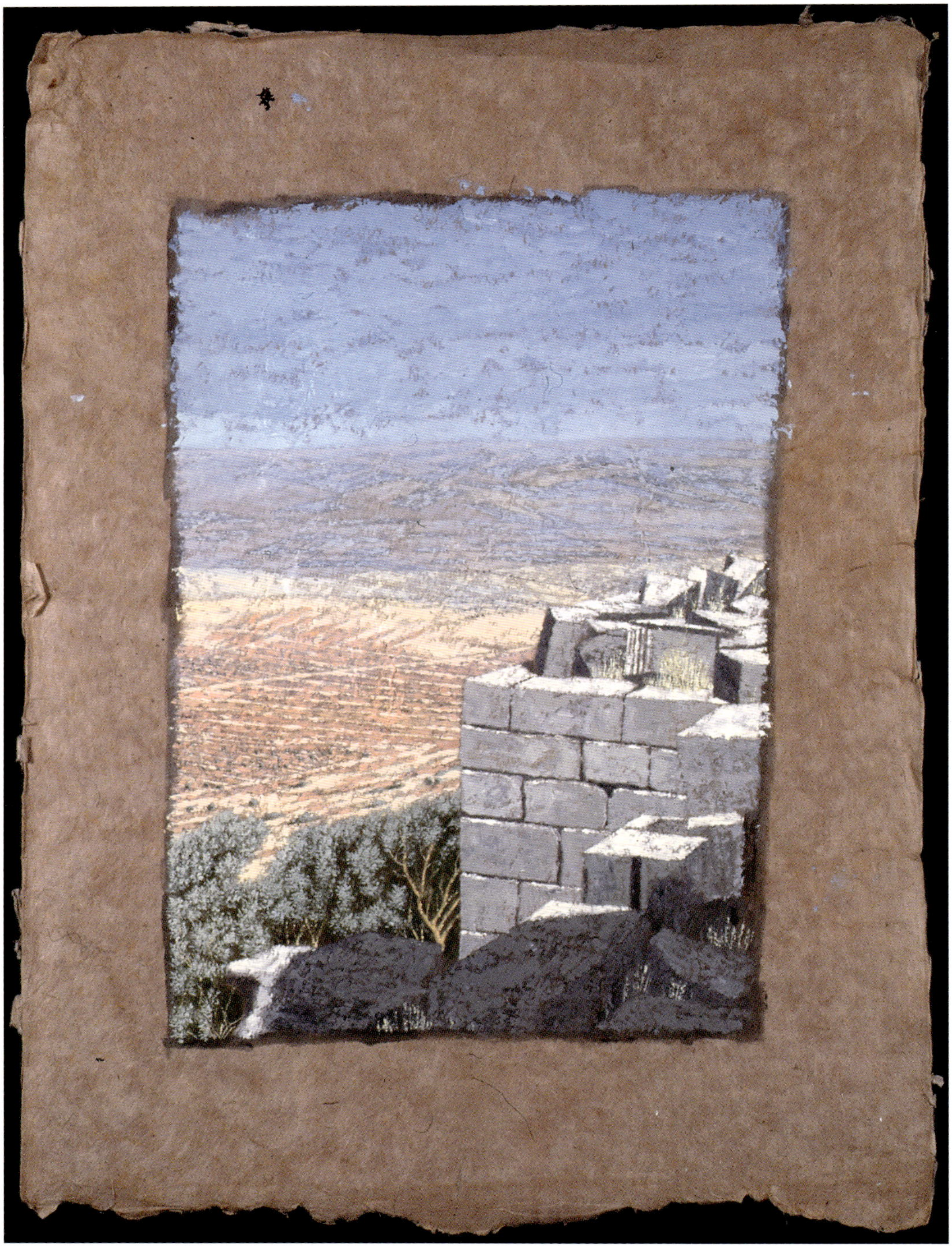

The View from Telanissus II (1998)

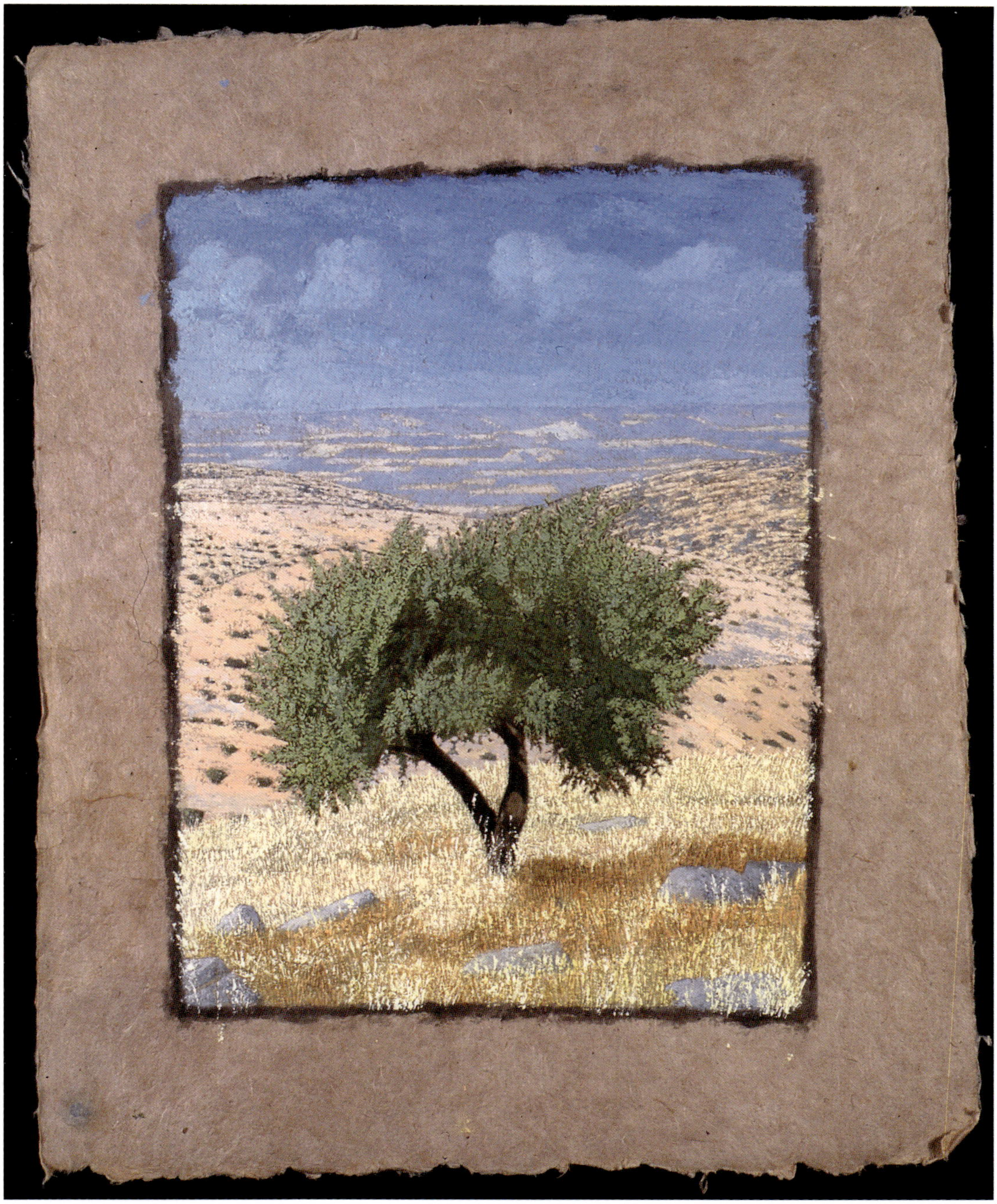

The View from Telanissus I (1998)

The *View from Telanissus II* (1998) [p28], contrasting with the sublime of the blue and yellow distances. The *View from Telanissus I* (1998) [p29] displays a prickly juniper centring an entire landscape of roseate rocks and scrub, the foreground stained with purple and orange; the tree seems to carry on its double crown the blue-shadowed mountains of the distance. For those unfamiliar with Wagner's English work, this is a tree. For those who know that work, this is the tree of life set in the landscape of the crucifixion and one of his most impressive evocations of the intense light and heat of that landscape.

That landscape is also the setting for one of Wagner's clearer evocations of Poussin, *Ruth and Boaz* (2000) [p62]. His composition shares with Poussin's its diagonal axes traversing fields of wheat but, in a touching gesture, Ruth and Boaz bear the features of Wagner and his wife Anne. His second *Abraham and the Angels* (2002) is also set in the valley below the desert plateau. Here the ornamental foreground of the Bedouin camp with its carpet and cushions have an almost neo-Orientalist intricacy, but in the background the arid Syrian landscape and monumental cement works are as forbidding as the cooling towers/crematoria of *Menorah* [pp53–55]. Wagner has said, 'I have no explanation for why things happen; but I do celebrate trust. There are explanations. It is not meaningless chaos that confronts us every day.'[12] And the question of God's justice—of theodicy—is prominent in his work.

---

[12] Roger Wagner quoted in Godfrey Barker, 'An English Visionary of Genius', *Daily Telegraph*, January 31, 1991

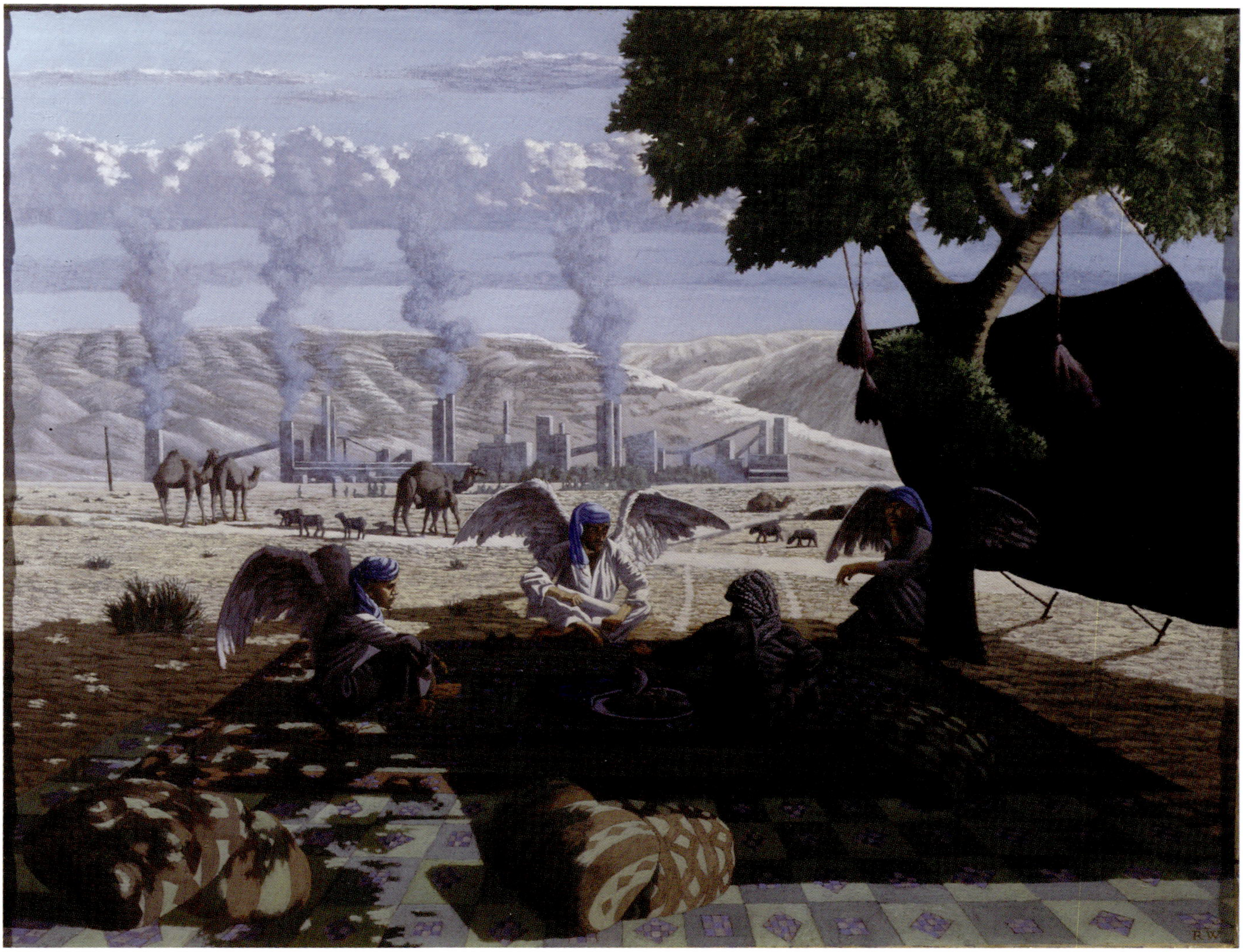

Abraham and the Angels (2002)

Theodicy is, of course, the subject of the book of Job. But before turning to Job, I should like to make one further excursion from 12 Mount Place. It takes us past Lucy's and up onto Waltonwell Road, which descends to the flood plain. Following the towpath upstream, one passes before the village of Binsey towards Wolvercote village and the ruins of Godstow Abbey. Between Binsey and the river bend labelled on the map as Black Jack's Hole stand a number of huge poplars, hybrids of the rare native black poplar. Their situation is very like that of the oak shown in the fourth woodcut of *Fire Sonnets*. In this area stood the aspens whose felling in 1879 was lamented in Gerard Manley Hopkins's famous poem 'Binsey Poplars', and *Binsey Poplar* is the title shared by a number of Wagner's paintings.

Binsey Poplar 1 (2004) might in fact be better described as a Godstow poplar; it stands in a field behind the ruins of Godstow Abbey. Among Wagner's more admired predecessors in the lyrical depiction of English landscape is Paul Nash. And one of the more striking aspects of Nash's painting is the degree of abstraction that he practised in his landscapes. He painted his *Landscape of the Summer Solstice* (1943) from the outskirts of Oxford at Boar's Hill using binoculars. It shows the Iron Age hill fort at Wittenham Clumps, downstream of Oxford near the village of Dorchester. The stand of beeches on the higher of the two hills is portrayed in this work almost like a single mushroom with multiple stalks. Both Rupert Martin and Wagner admired the work, and Wittenham Clumps joined their 'elected' landscapes. Wagner's compositional skills allow him, like Paul Nash, to incorporate a high degree of abstraction into a naturalist representation. In *Binsey Poplar 1*, the top of a hedge acts as a foreground repoussoir. The eye is then led toward the tree down what are effectively the lines of perspective in the clayey furrows, deliberately set slightly off-centre. These are intersected by the long shadows that fall across them, staging the eye's arrival at the tree. In the form of the tree itself we feel the presence of precise geometries: a triangle, an oval and the circle formed by the bushes (brambles and hawthorns *in situ*) at the base of the trunk.

In symbolic terms, what is significant is the absence of any further world beyond that defined by the flat horizon. In this image, a tree seems to occupy all the space between earth and heaven and takes us implicitly to other trees painted by Wagner, notably *A Tree of Life II* (1999). Though the graceful upward arc of the limbs is entirely typical of black poplars, *Binsey Poplar I* is a symbolic composition of supreme naturalistic conviction. The tree is completely isolated from the world and the dark evening light is dramatic and even menacing (enhanced by the stippling effect of the Nepalese paper). Its stooping embrace of the bushes at its feet has echoes of Piero's *Madonna del Parto at Monterchi*, but in its melancholy it is reminiscent of a Crucifixion.

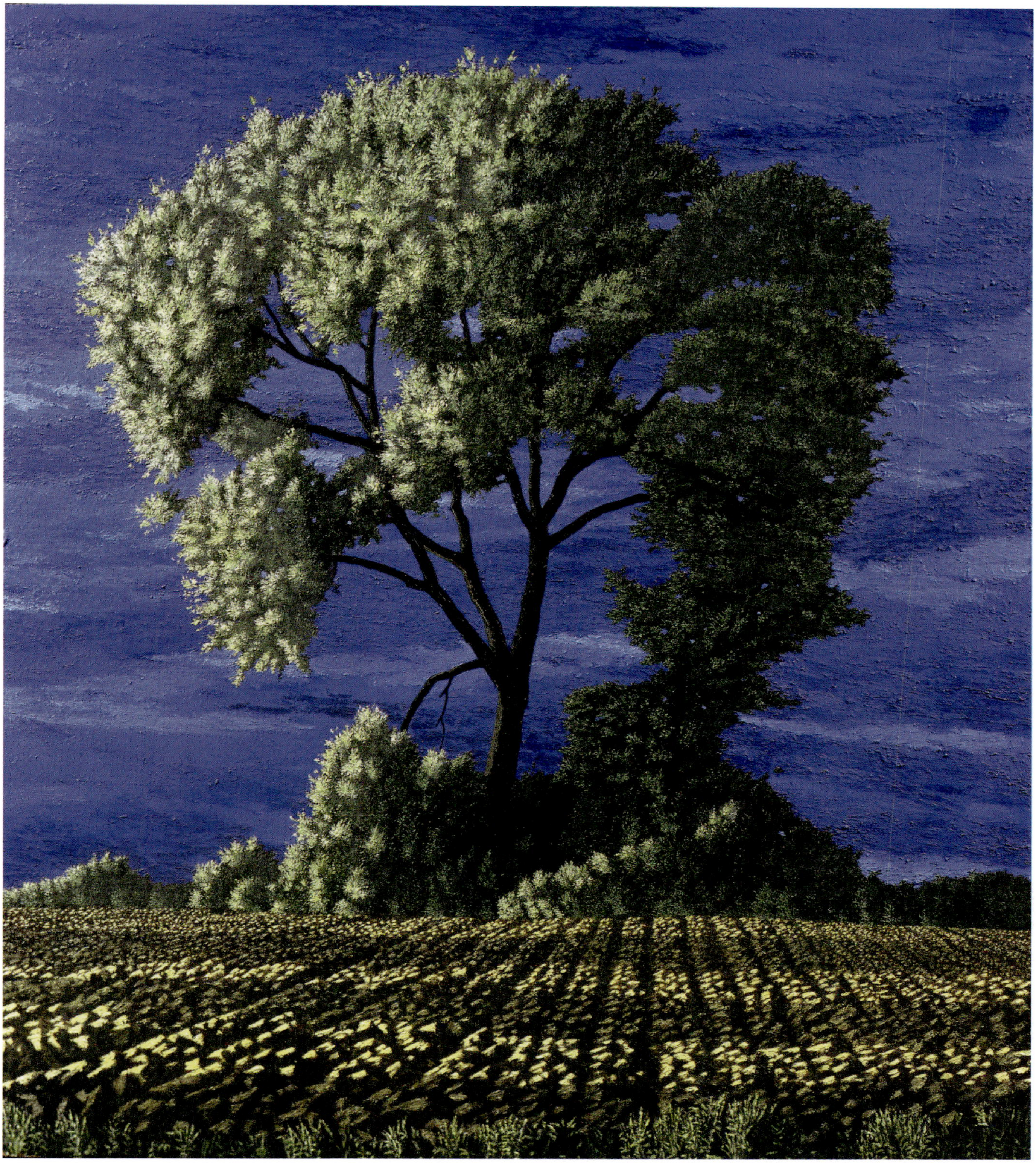

Binsey Poplar I (2004)

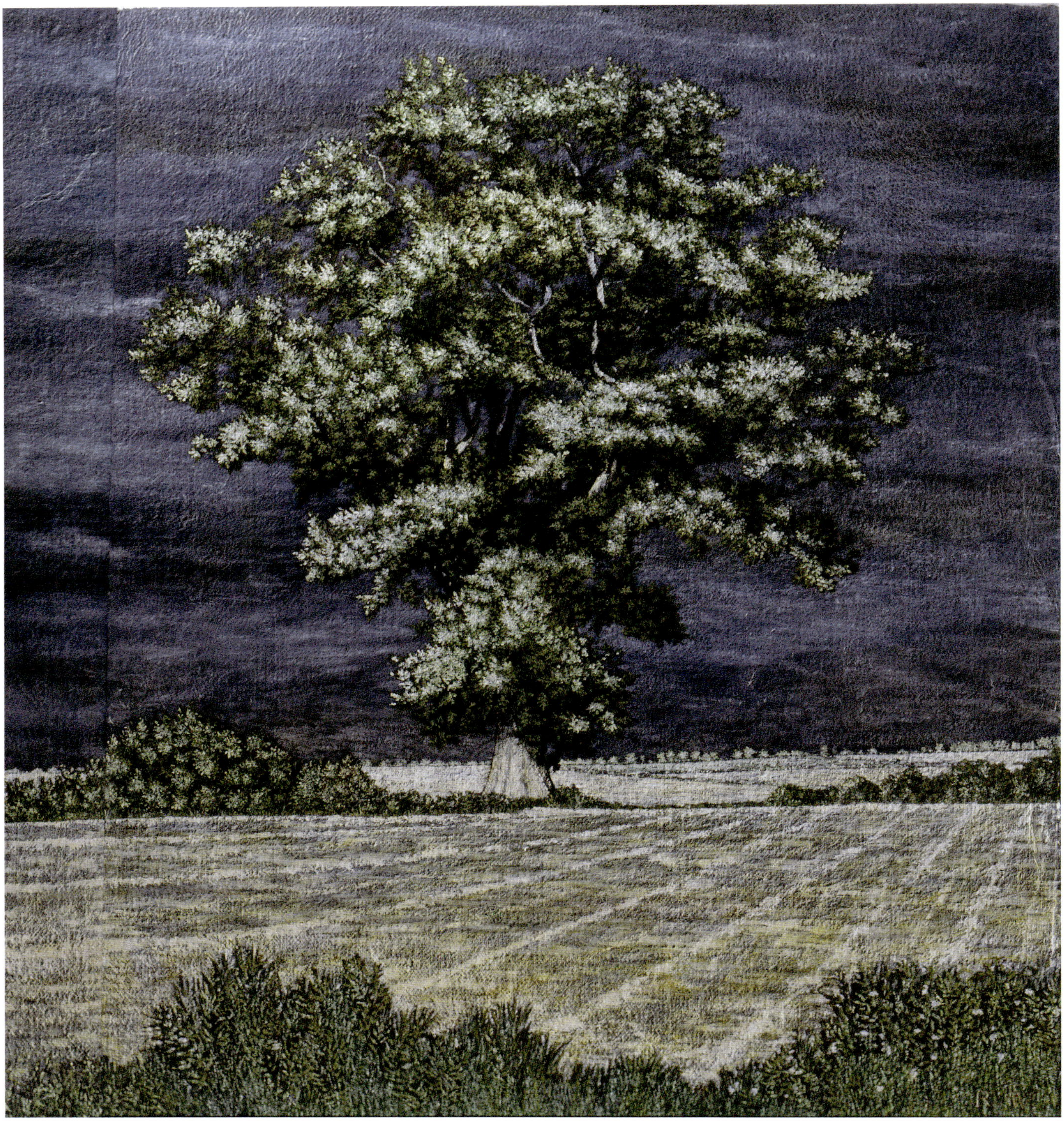

Cazalet Oak (2004)

Wagner has created something of a specialization in trees. A memorable exhibition at Lady Margaret Hall, Oxford (2004) was entirely devoted to trees—some familiar to the Oxford dweller and others, such as the *Cazalet Oak* (2004), less local. These works are, in every sense, portraits. The explicit formalism of Wagner's style—shown, for example, in the studied parallels of shadows and clouds in *Oak Tree with Sheep* (2004) [p37]—is combined to magisterial effect with a painstakingly detailed approach to the depiction of leaves and branches. The slightly dry effect of mixed media on Nepalese paper seems paradoxically to enhance the effects of light. The *Strancally Turkey Oak* (2006) [p38], a vast turkey oak with an almost beech-like canopy, was commissioned by the owners of Strancally Castle rather as one might commission a family portrait. It opens its magnificent limbs over the countryside as if in benediction, standing beside the entrance to the walled park. A comparison here might be the protective cloak of the Madonna in Piero's *Madonna della Misericordia*.

More typical is *Oak Tree* (2004) [p39], a painting clearly related to the oak tree of *The Harvest* [p17]. The curve of horizon gives a strong impression that it is a tree of life or world tree. It is as if we were witnessing an extraordinary, centennial time-lapse sequence; in its sheer vibrancy, the tree seems to have arisen from the acorn before our very eyes in a burst of cosmic energy finishing in this majestic, stilled pirouette. At the same time it is clearly subject to the processes of time and age, its bare broken boughs gesturing at its mortality. Behind it, the estuary marshland of the Suffolk coast is as if a department of the sky, with whose swirling cloud-lines it seems to meld. This is as much world tree, Yggdrasil, as a tree of life. The powerful impression of energy takes us into the eternal present, into the moment that is always coming into being, at once all movement and an entire absence of movement. This is the territory of the *via negativa*, of the fusion of self and universe that immerses the soul in love—in Wagner's understanding, God's love.

The notion of the tree of life is so rich as to more or less defy explanation. It is at once the prop of the sky, part of the structure of earth and heaven, the 'wood of life' of the Apocalypse; but it is also a metaphor for Christ as the non-material structure of heaven and earth, and as such it is a metaphor for the literal cross on which Christ was crucified. It leads us, too, toward the *Leggenda della vera croce* as told in Piero's supreme achievement in the apse of the basilica of San Francesco at Arezzo. The *Oak Tree, Snape* (2004) [p36] and *The Ocean in a Tree* (1984) are clearly related to *Fire Sonnets,* 'IV':

> And that exulting love which made all things
> Whose laughter is the ocean in a tree
> That rustles like a thousand angels' wings
> Stirred by a wind no human eye can see,
> Breathes love into a world he would inspire
> In winds that flame with pentecostal fire.

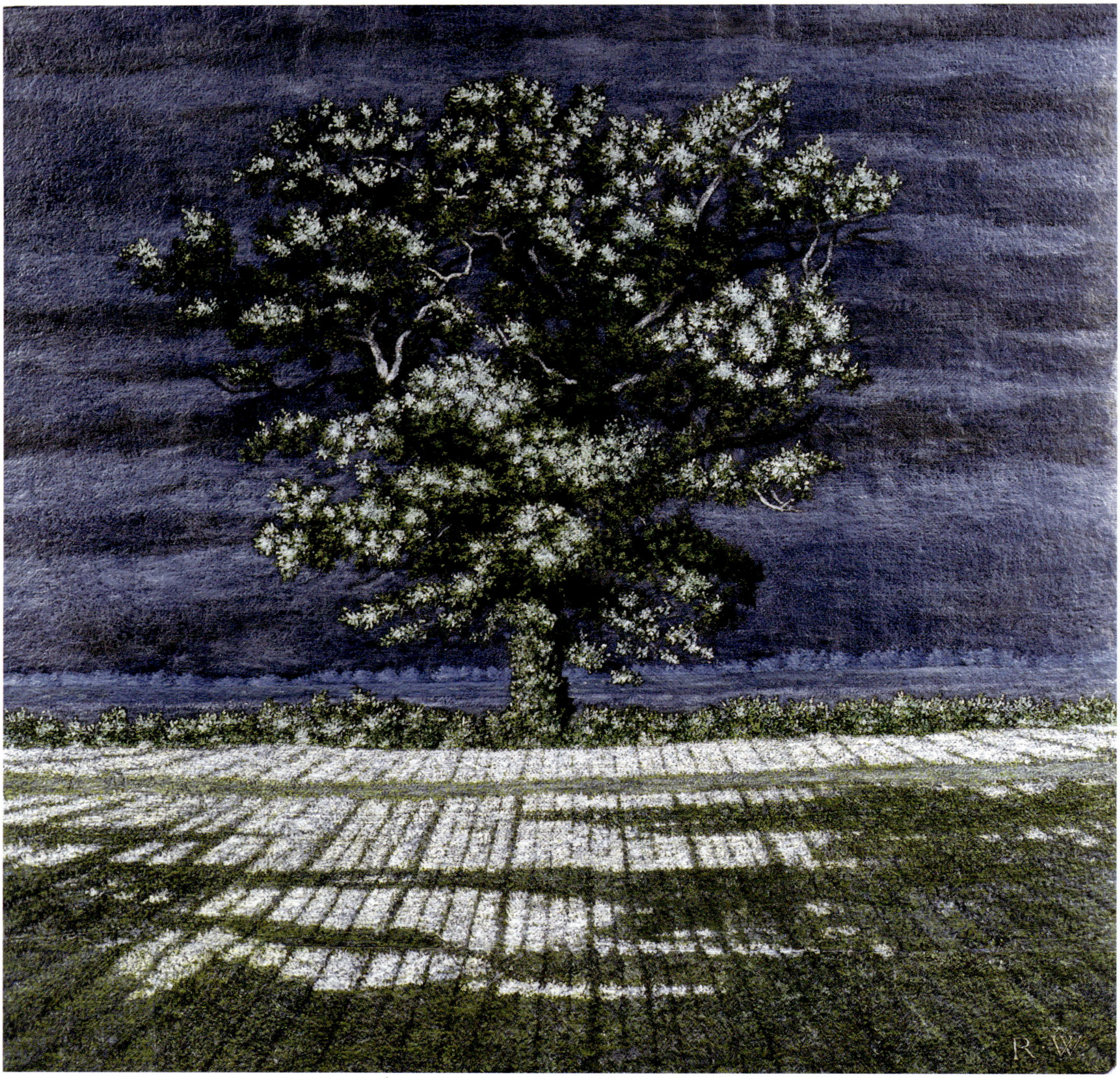

Oak Tree, Snape (2004)

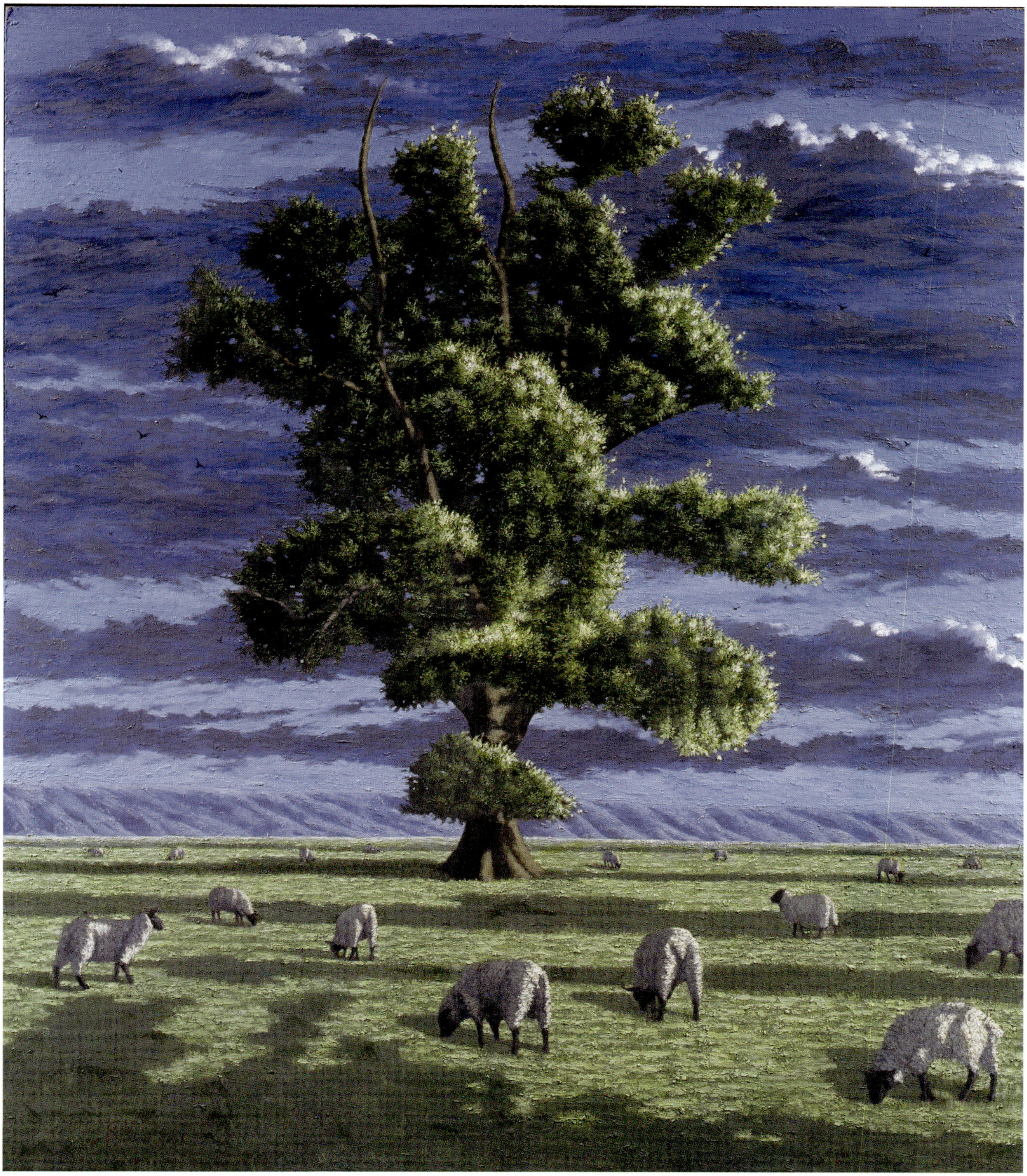

Oak Tree with Sheep (2004)

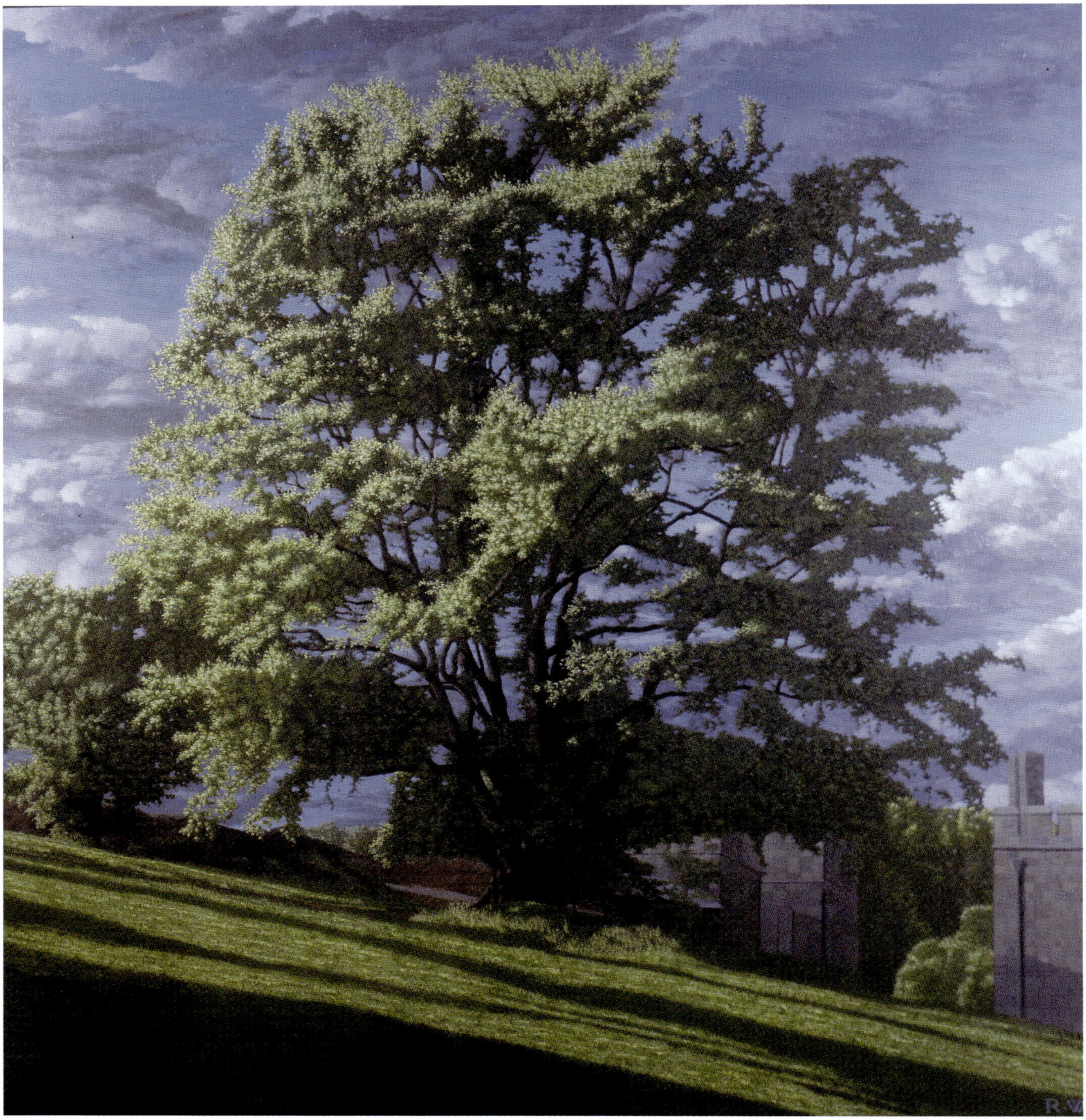

Strancally Turkey Oak (2006)

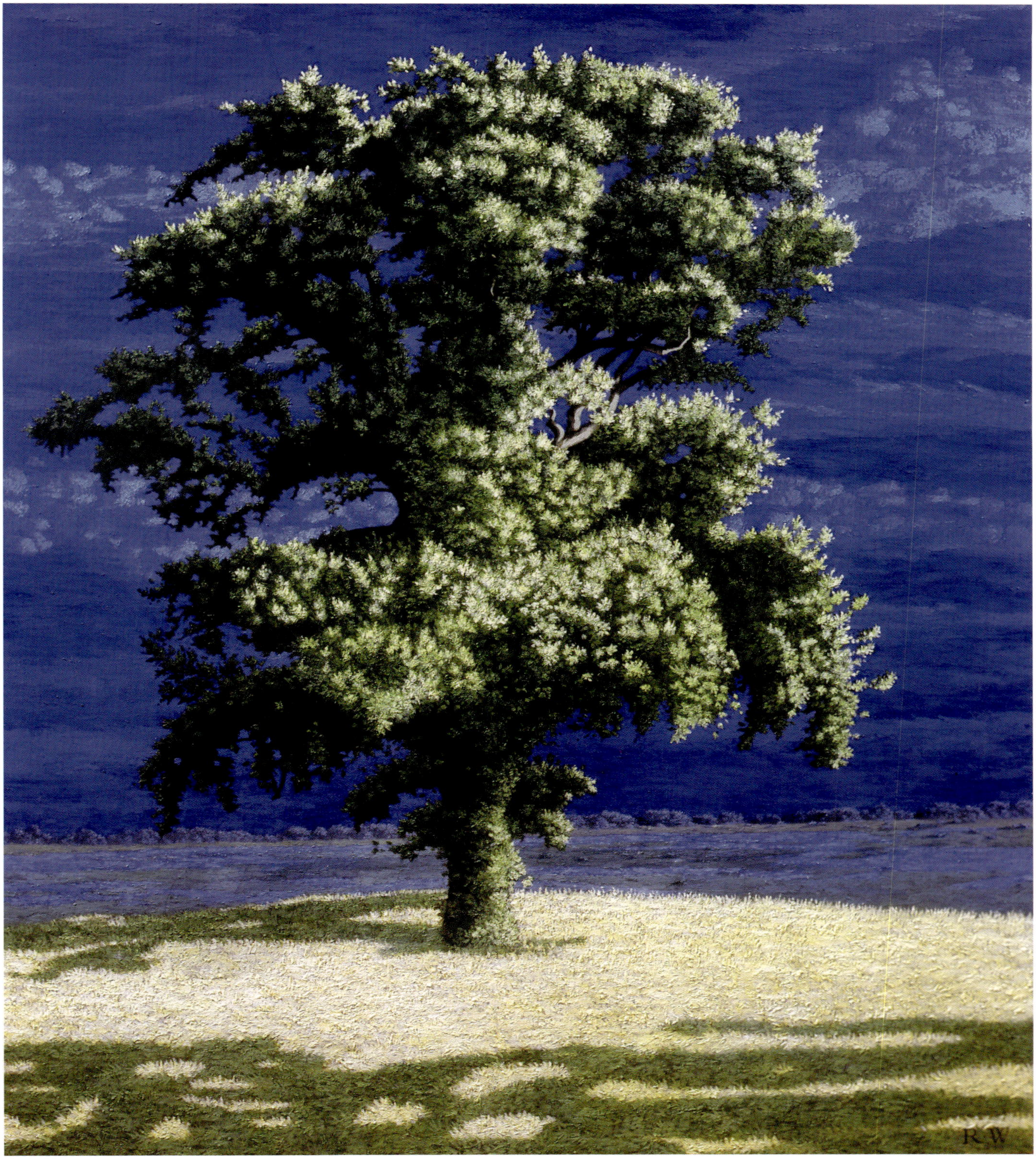

Oak Tree (2004)

A concern with construction is a constant in Wagner's art. Beauty, we have said, is never meaningless in his work. We see him in the versions of his *Dartmoor Crucifixion* (2007) working towards a naturalistic solution to the extreme symmetry of his conception. Here the telegraph posts that form the three crosses are necessarily superimposed on trees conveniently growing in front of the hedgerow that follows the dark base of the hills. On the hills, the patchwork of fields is neatly sown into parcels that assert the convergences of perspective. In the foreground, the sheep form an apex whose point is the base of the cross, while the shadows form a further cross whose point of intersection is the centre of the ovine pyramid. The clouds echo this St Andrew's cross as if the light were the intersection of several spotlights, the dramatic lighting being implicitly that of the crucifixion. It nevertheless takes place on that most banal of human artefacts, the telegraph pole, well below the ambit of this theatre. Here then is an artifice of symmetry. The cunning of the composition is to disguise its artifice in approximation while making of unnatural artifice a metaphor of the supernatural.

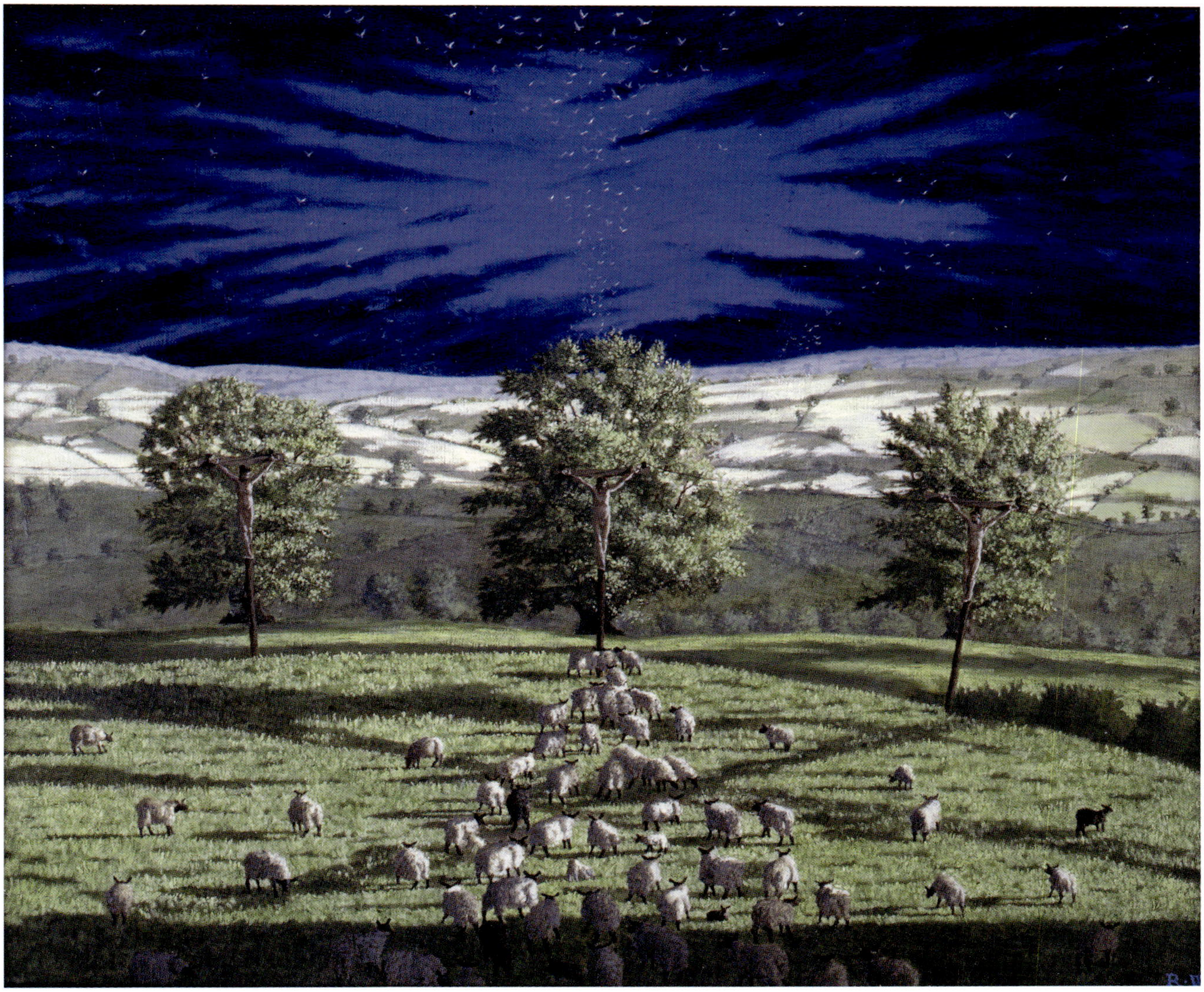

Dartmoor Crucifixion (2007)

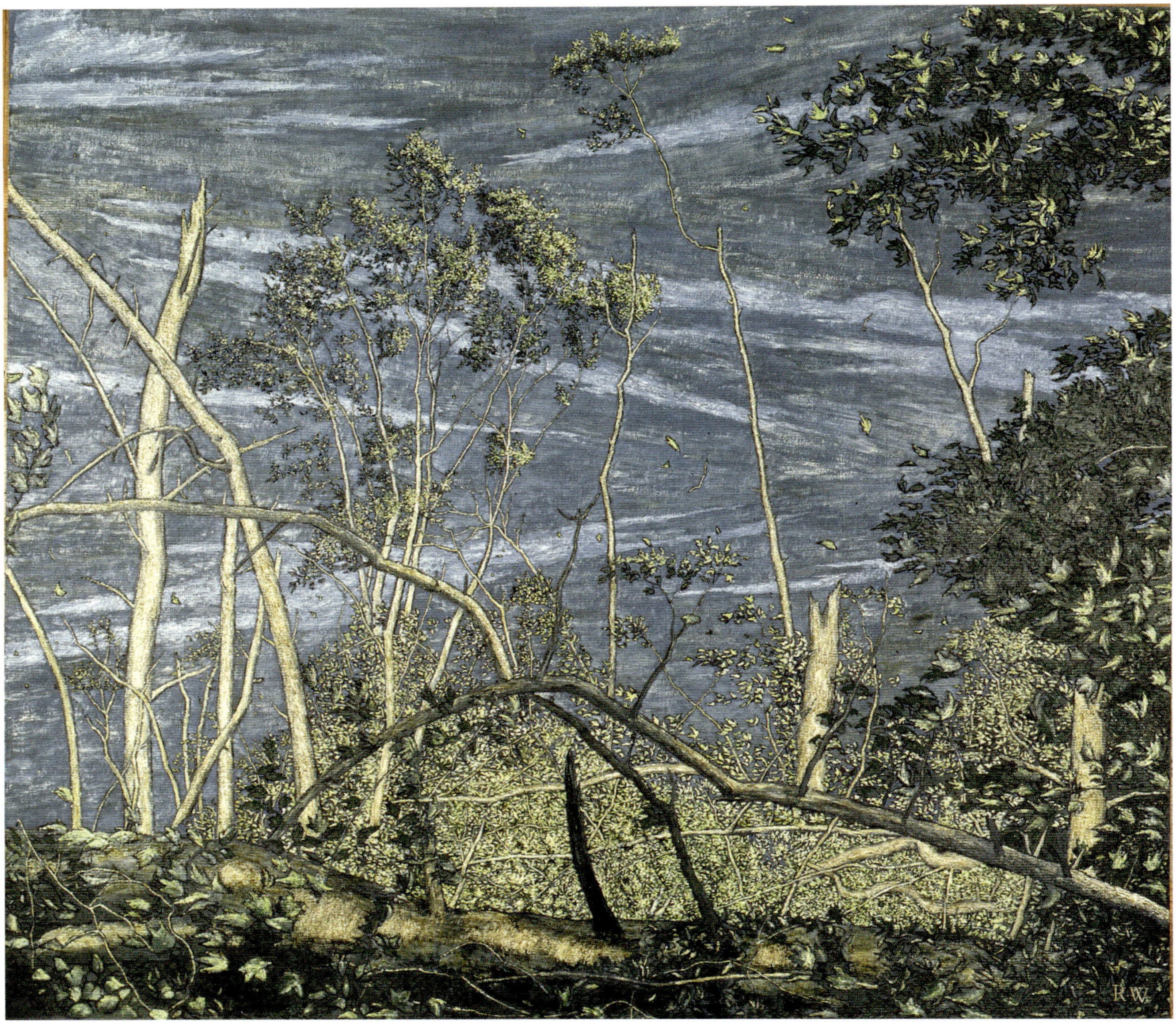

See What Desolations (1989)

We have seen that trees have a major role in Wagner's oeuvre and the hurricane of 1989 consequently inspired a very beautiful set of paintings lamenting the execution wrought by that storm. Among the finest of these images is *See What Desolations* (1989), which takes its title from Psalm 46: 'Come, behold the works of the Lord, What desolations he hath made in the earth'. It is a fine example of the compositional skills that give Wagner's work such authority. The line of straggly trunks left upright by the tornado form a circle within which the viewer is implicitly placed. Above this line, a single branch reaches up to the apex of the painting. Reading right to left across this line, the eye is drawn down the closely-observed dark sycamore leaves to the base of the painting, where a larger tree lies almost like a crucifix, as if thrown on its back with its arms open. From the bottom right-hand corner an indirect diagonal bisects the lower half of the painting to meet the frame midway up the left-hand side, whence an implied diagonals bisects the upper half. Two darker branches at the lower centre of the painting form an arrow pointing towards the central vertical. The chevron formations in the sky predominantly point toward the right but the wind is clearly coming from the right, raising the sycamore branches and tearing off the leaves that float across this landscape. In the centre lies the confused mass of fallen limbs and desiccating leaves, each carefully picked out at its meeting with the light. The junction and gradation of tones here is particularly fine.

Psalm 46 states that the Lord is 'a very present help in trouble' and that the Israelites will not therefore be troubled 'though the mountains shake'. The combination of natural disaster and war foreshadowed in that psalm restores us to the issue of theodicy and to a part of Oxford that entered Wagner's life somewhat later than Port Meadow and 12 Mount Place. It is a little chapel called Bartlemas on a lane off East Oxford's Cowley Road. The chapel was once used as a cowshed, but was built as chapel to

Oxford's leper house, just outside the city boundary. Leprosy is a perfect example of natural injustice. Only 3 per cent of humanity is susceptible to this disfiguring disease and contagion is only by prolonged contact. Yet there are still some 20 million cases in the world of which less than 20 per cent have access to treatment. Most of the remainder are still isolated, as they were in European lazar houses.

The series of paintings that Wagner chose to exhibit at Bartlemas Chapel tells the story of Job. The absorption of acrylic by the thick, handmade Nepalese paper has distorted the irregular torn oblongs and squares within their frames, as though the paper were reverting to its plant components. On the cosmic blue backgrounds of the larger paintings, birds adumbrate the flight of angels around the throne of God. In each painting, half-ovals above and below a central roundel or square contain further roundels. The dialogue between Job and God is thus punctuated by the proofs that God adduces. We do not see the entire story of Job, which is a profound questioning of the theodicy. Job is wealthy and content and praises the Lord; the devil questions whether Job does so out of true conviction or out of satisfaction with his state. The Lord therefore permits the devil to reduce Job to abject poverty. His comforters try to persuade Job that God's considerations are beyond human justice. And when God does speak, his arguments, as Wagner says, are not 'forensic'[13] but akin to the argument from creation: vivid vignettes of the immensity and unpredictability of the created world. And Job acknowledges that he can have no complaint against such a God. Yet the acknowledgement is sufficient to restore him to his wealth, as though faith must precede justice. The exhibition was accompanied by a performance of the Book of Job, in which Wagner played one of the comforters.

As Wagner explains in his book *Out of the Whirlwind: Illustrations to the Book of Job* (1997), the pictures were inspired by 'the memory of medieval stained glass with its leaded roundels and multiplicity of images contained within a single frame'. The functions of medieval stained glass were to impart or sustain the conviction of faith by dramatic coloured light such as the worshipper would see nowhere else. And this in turn is the task attempted by Wagner's Job series. Job is pictured almost like an Indian sadhu, naked but for his loincloth, sitting astonished as God (green-robed) seeds the sky with the Milky Way [pp46-47] and shows the boundaries he has set to the ocean. Vast forks of lightning are seen over the green continents, while raven and wild ass go about their unfathomable business. Finally, the humpback Leviathan leaps out of the water like a dolphin [p48]. In the last of these cameos, the Lord lifts up Job's face and they finally see eye to eye [p49]. The burden of this series is to maintain the dialogue and logic of the interaction while imbuing God's successive proofs with a vividness akin to miracle—and it sustains the challenge.

---

[13] Roger Wagner, *Out of the Whirlwind: Illustrations to the Book of Job* (Carlisle: Solway, 1997), no page numbers

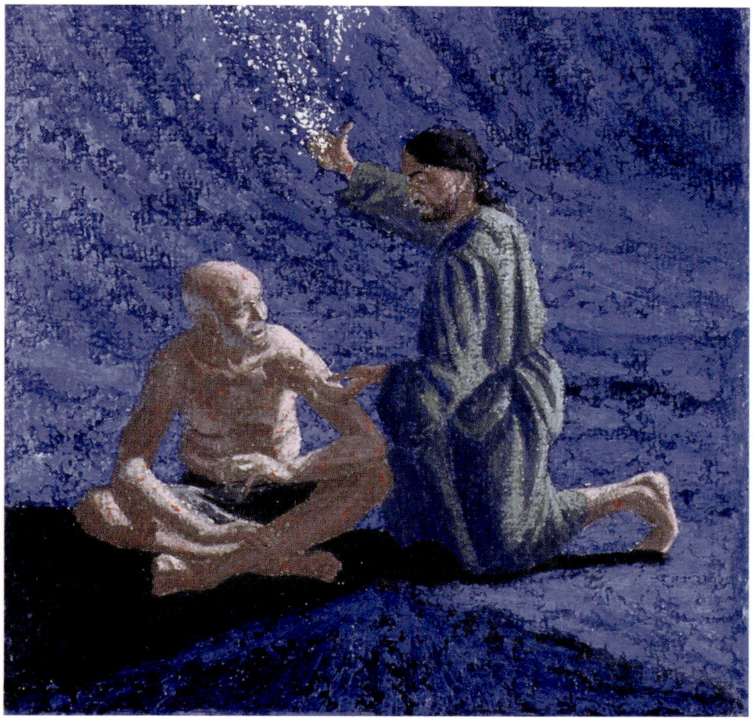

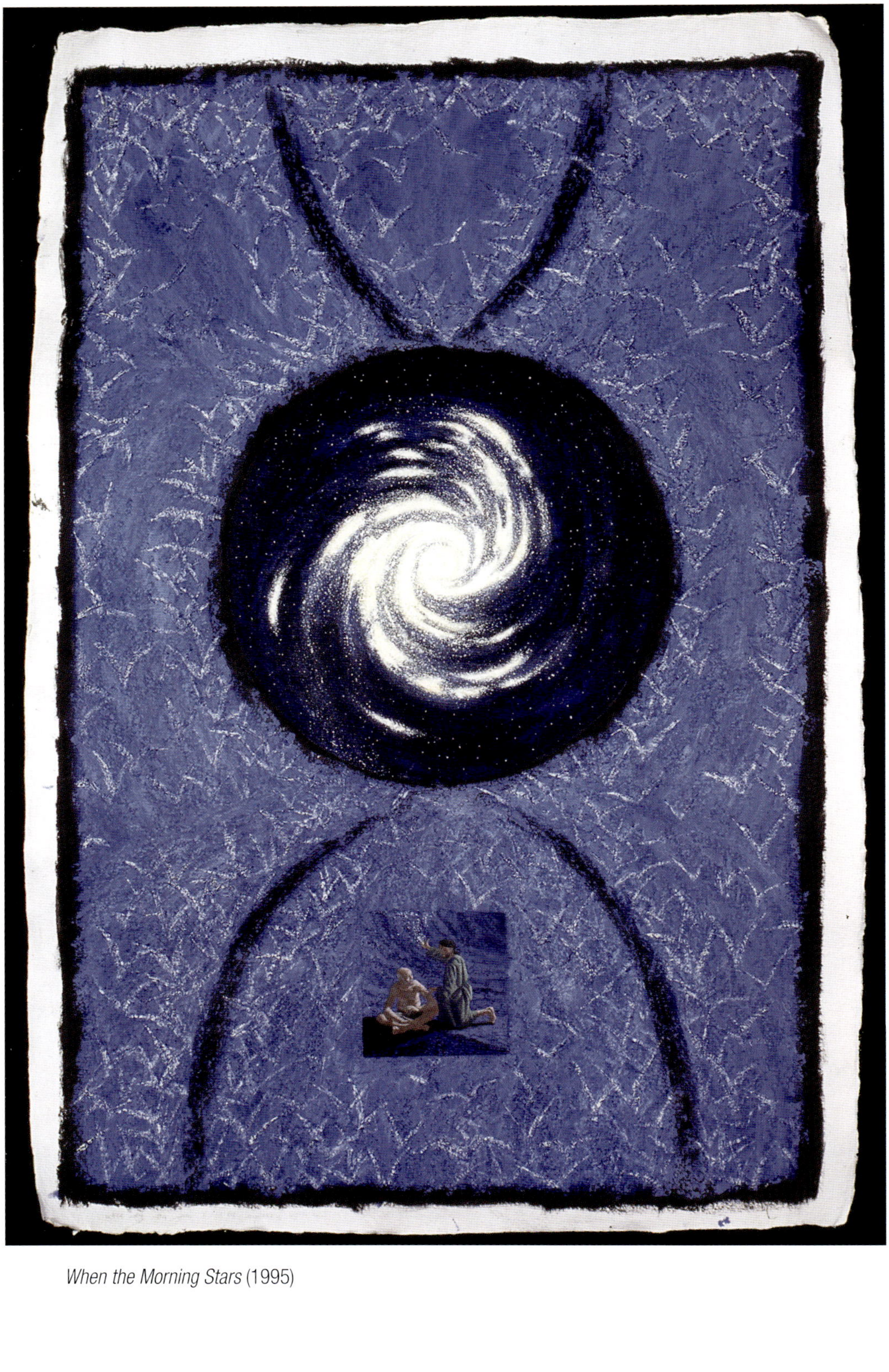

When the Morning Stars (1995)

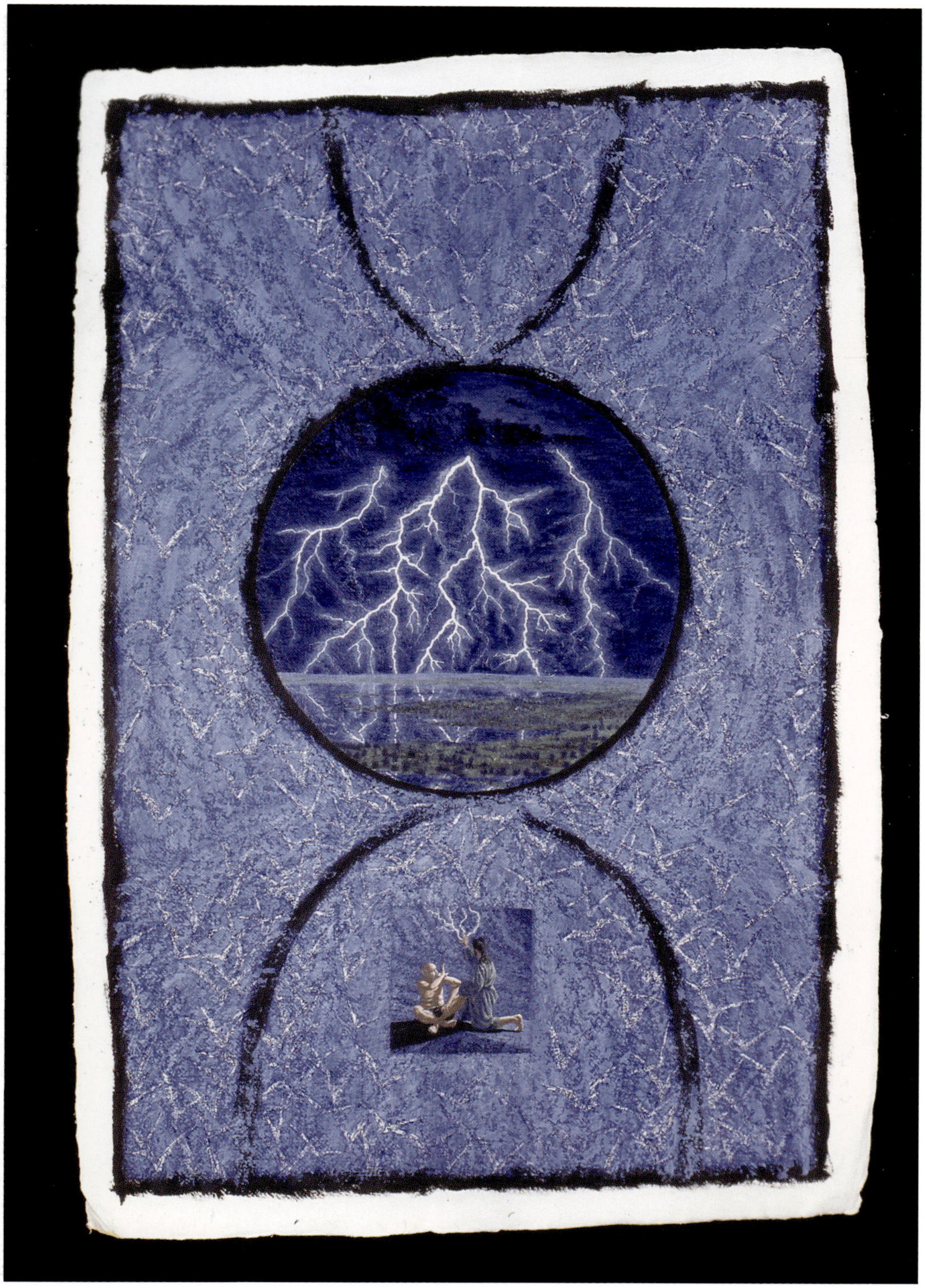

The Lightning Bolts (1995)

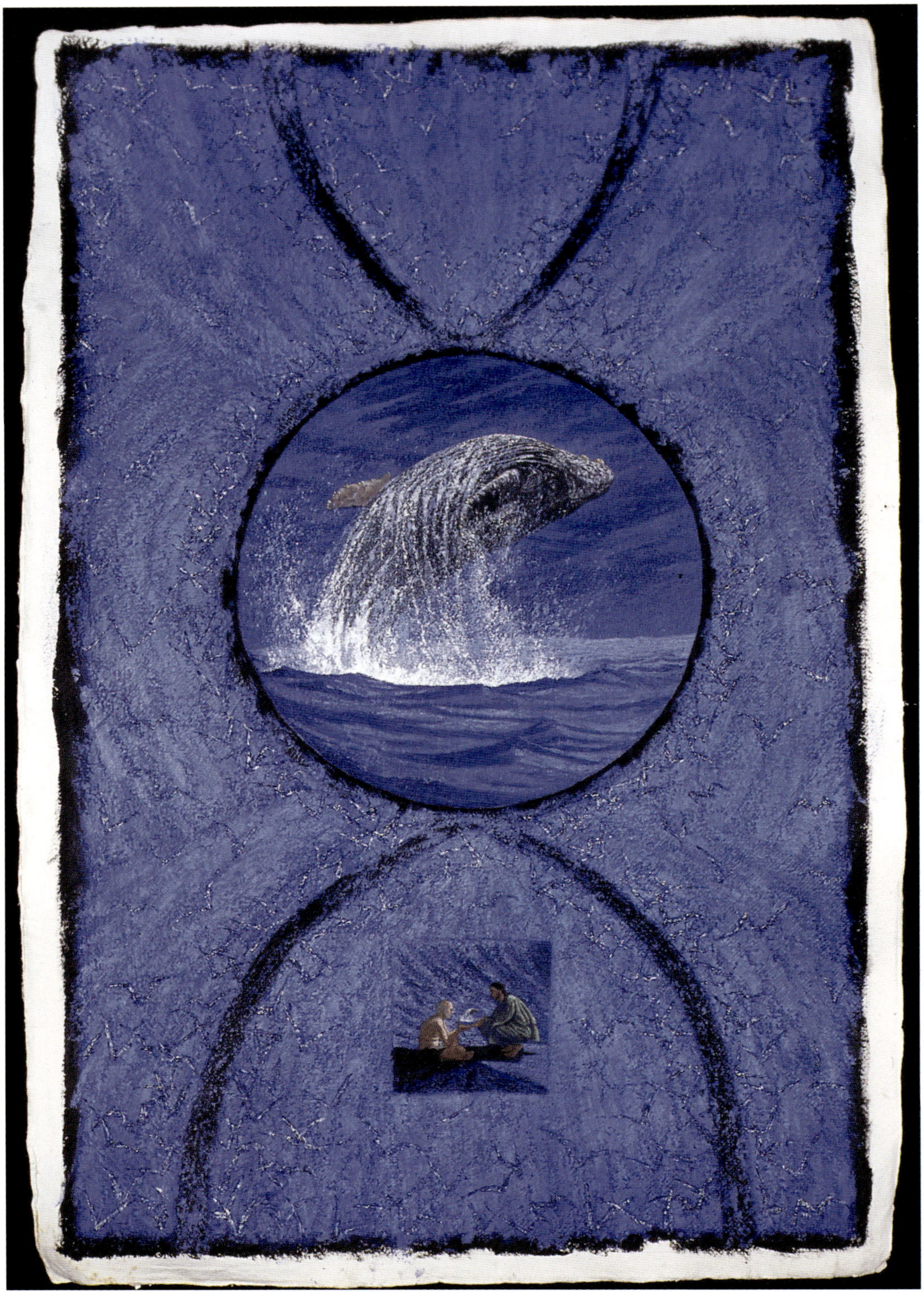

Leviathan (1995)

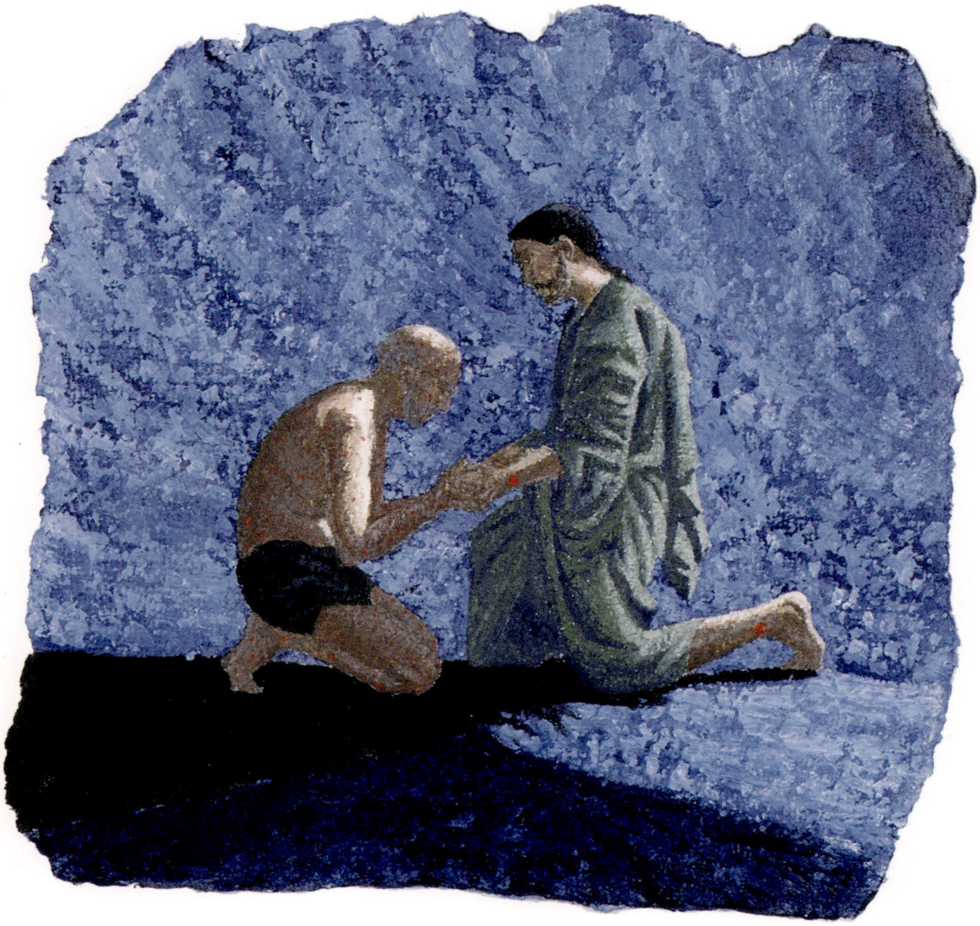

'My ears had heard of you but now my eyes have seen you' (1995)

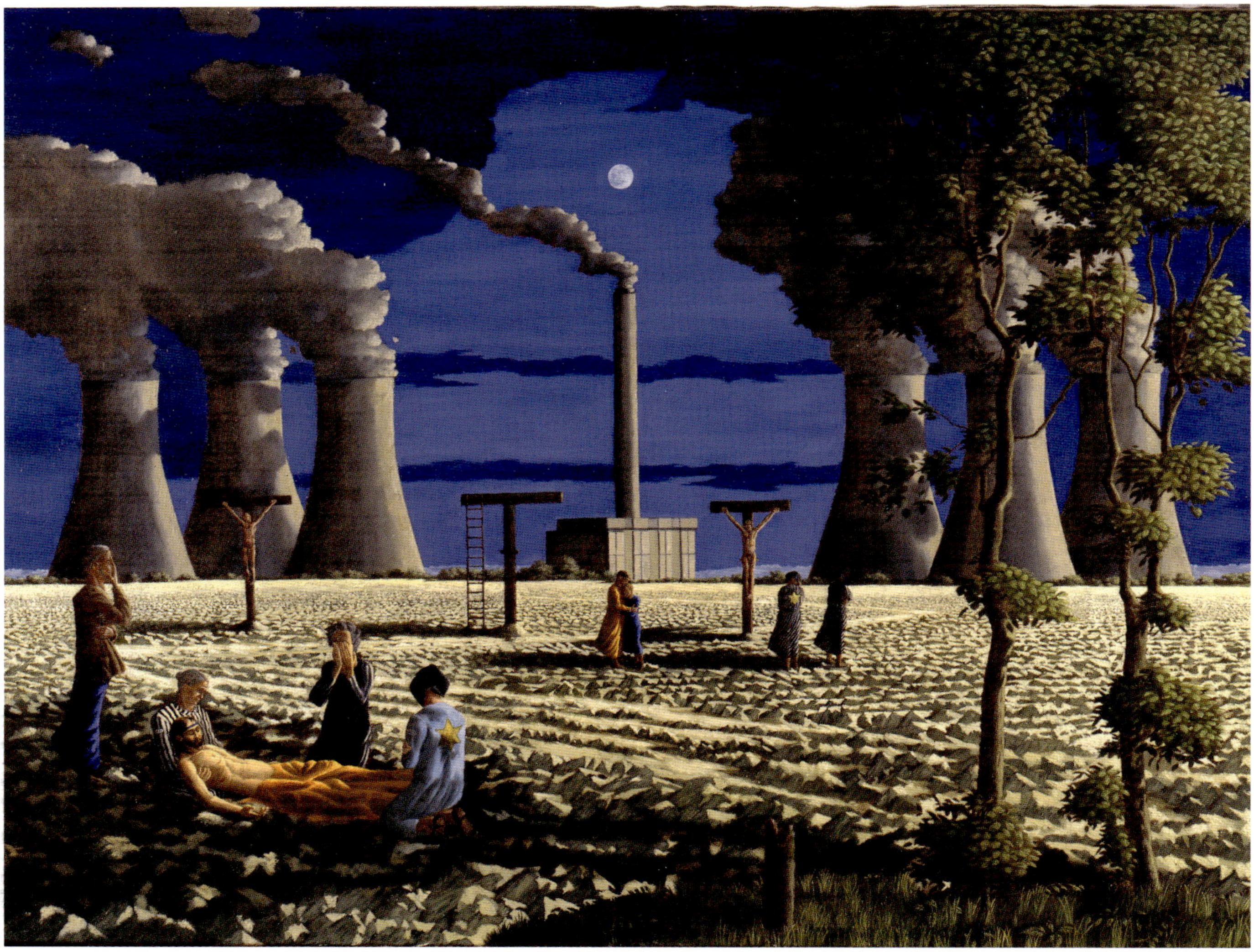

Surely He Has Borne Our Griefs (1989)

To speak of theodicy in Wagner's work is necessarily to evoke two of his most impressive and powerful canvases. They may also be read as a commentary on what technological and economic progress mean. The two paintings centre on a non-Christian symbol, the Jewish menorah. This seven-branched candelabra was kept burning in the Temple in Jerusalem till its destruction and is therefore symbolic of the presence of God. The first of these is a Deposition, *Surely He Has Borne Our Griefs* (1989). It is a deliberately monumental work: the three bare crosses stand in front of Didcot power station, whose two sets of three cooling towers and single central chimney together make up the Menorah. In the left foreground, two of the mourners around the dead Christ wear the striped garb of the Nazi concentration camps and another the yellow star imposed on Jews before they were sent to the camps. The bare acres of ploughed land lead the eye across the painting from the trees in the right foreground to the axial chimney of the turbine hall set beneath the full moon. In this version, Wagner's symbolic powers perhaps outran his redoubtable compositional skills and the canvas as a whole is too empty.

In *Menorah* (1993) [pp53–55] the challenges of the composition are triumphantly resolved. The angle is steeper. The light, as Richard Harries, former Bishop of Oxford, has observed, is 'nothing less than the light of judgement'.[1414] This is a Crucifixion, not a Deposition. The marl of the foreground is a glabrous, flooded desolation. The figures before the cross wear the sober clothing of Hasidic Jewry. The turbine hall is shrouded in cloud, simultaneously masking and accentuating the symmetries. And the figures here testify to the reality of massacre and genocide. Some are borrowed from a celebrated photograph by Dmitri Baltermants—*Grief, Kerch, Crimea*—in which the thaw has exposed the bodies of victims of the Wehrmacht. Others looked out of our own newspapers in the late nineties from the ethnic cleansing in former Yugoslavia.

---

[14] The Rt Revd Richard Harries, *The Passion in Art* (Aldershot: Ashgate, 2004), p134

In his memoir *Night*, Elie Wiesel remembers two scenes, the first immediately after his arrival at Auschwitz, when a lorry-load of babies was emptied into the vast outdoor pyres. The sight stripped him of his faith. In the second, the inmates of the Buna factory camp were assembled to witness the death of an angelic boy condemned to hang with his accomplices for planning an insurrection. The boy is too light to have his neck broken by the fall and hangs in mortal agony for half an hour. Then and later, when the inmates are forced to contemplate the dead body, Wiesel hears a voice asking, 'Where is God? Where is he?' Wiesel is inclined to answer 'Here He is—hanging on this gallows.'[15] For the Jews in the concentration camps, it might seem that the title Chosen People could only be ironic. Yet in Jesus' last words on the cross, *'Eloi, Eloi, lama sabachthani'* ('My God, My God, why hast thou forsaken me?), we hear the same despair. And suddenly a transformation is effected. The Nazis placed the entire power of the industrial state at the service of mass murder, and the power of such technologies has grown unceasingly since the Second World War. Here in *Menorah* the titanic power and size of the power station hints at just such dangers. In Wagner's transformative art, the steam and smoke rising from its towers and chimney have become the chimneys of the crematoria on the Polish plains. The Jews of the concentration camps have become the Jewish Christians despairing at the foot of the cross and the angelic youth, a Christ dying again and again for the innocent as each new choice of humankind dictates. The literally evil-smelling smoke rises over the sodden plain to commemorate the 'inhumanity' of human action and again the Christ must die to redeem us.

It is clear from this astounding metaphor that Wagner's faith is able to accommodate not just the rural idylls of his elected landscape but the full weight of the twentieth century's 'progress' through totalitarianism and the capitalist logic and Utopian fallacies that presided over Stalag and Gulag alike.

---

[15] Elie Wiesel, *Night*, tr. Stella Rodway (London: Penguin, 1981), pp76–77

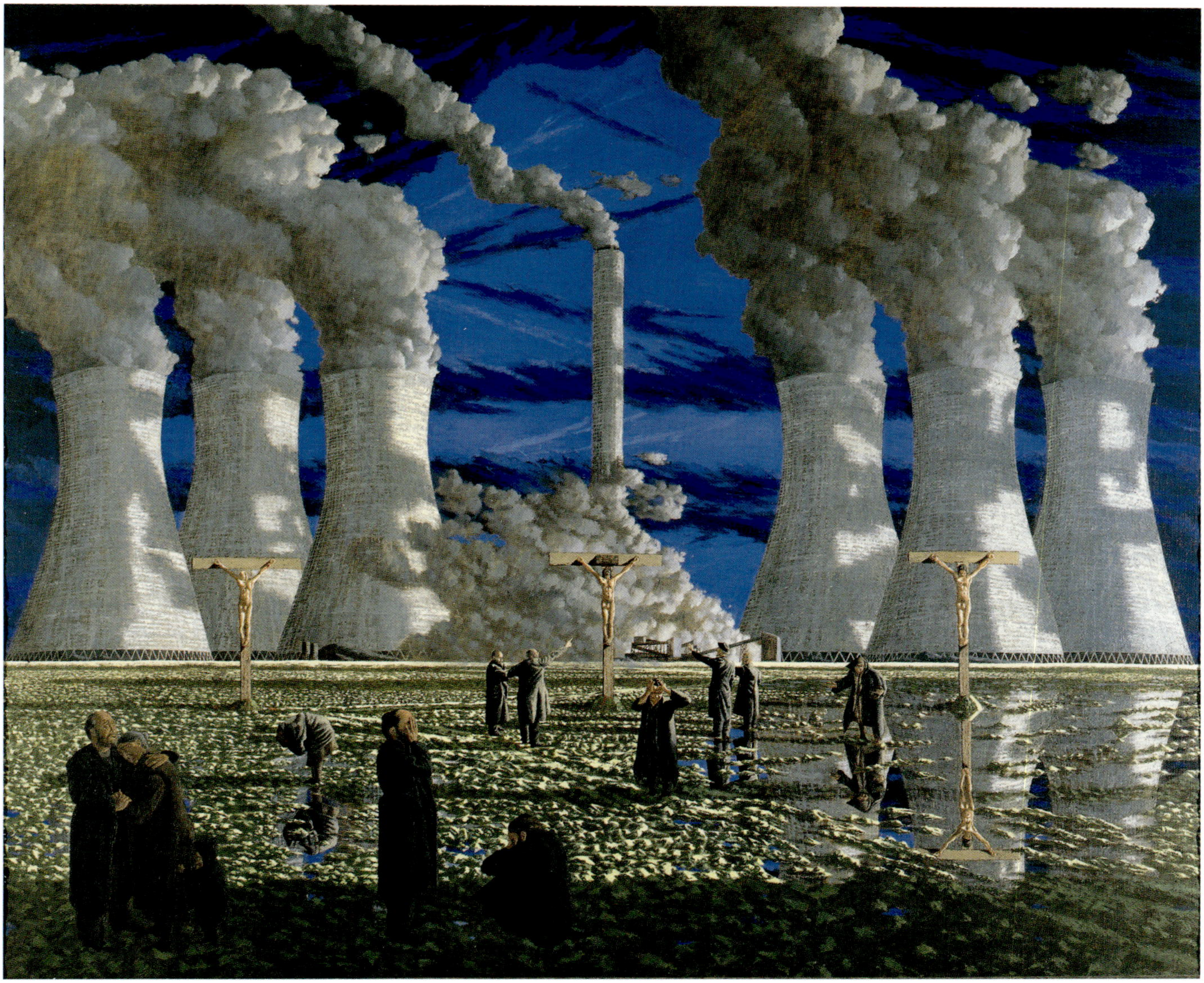

Menorah (1993)

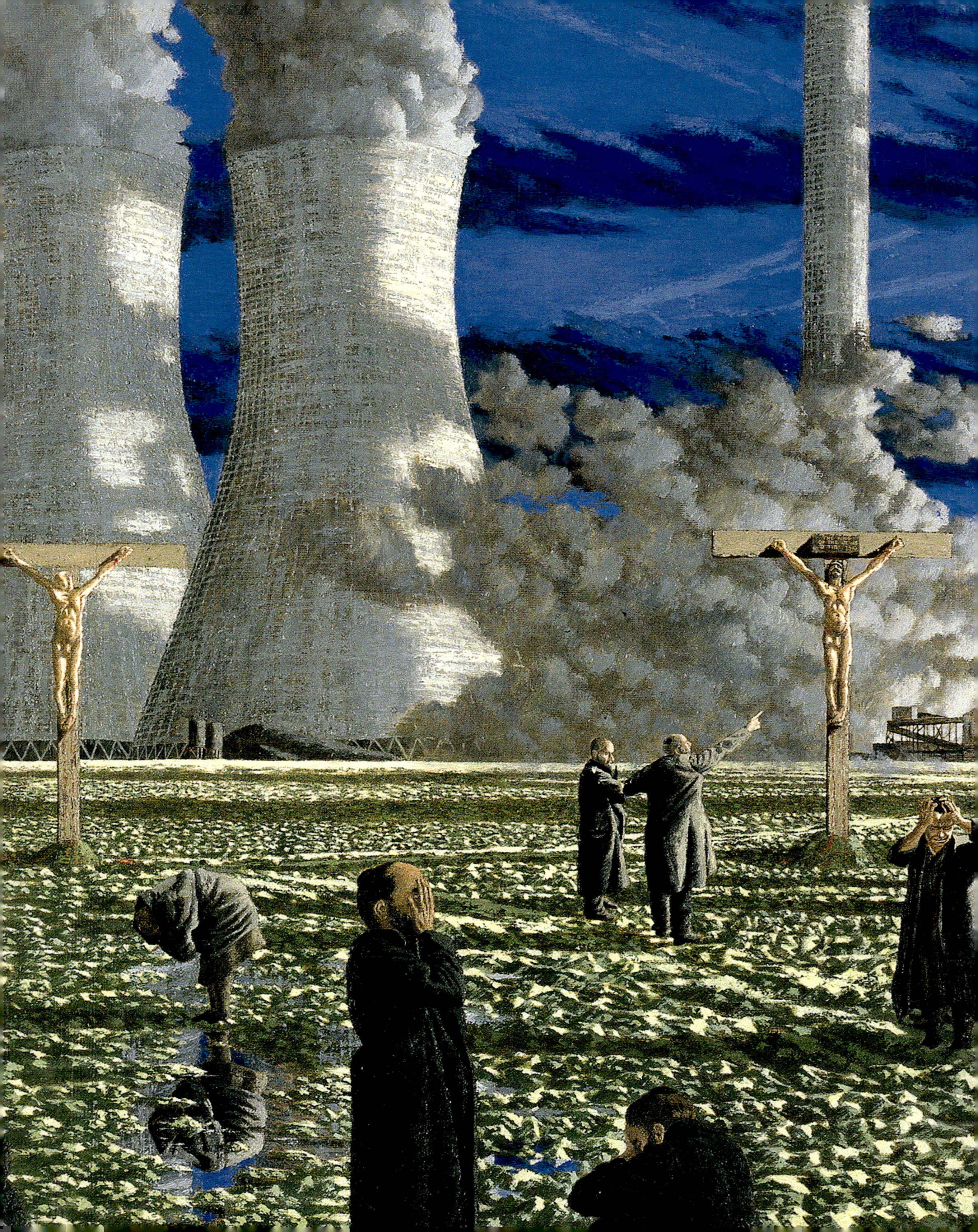

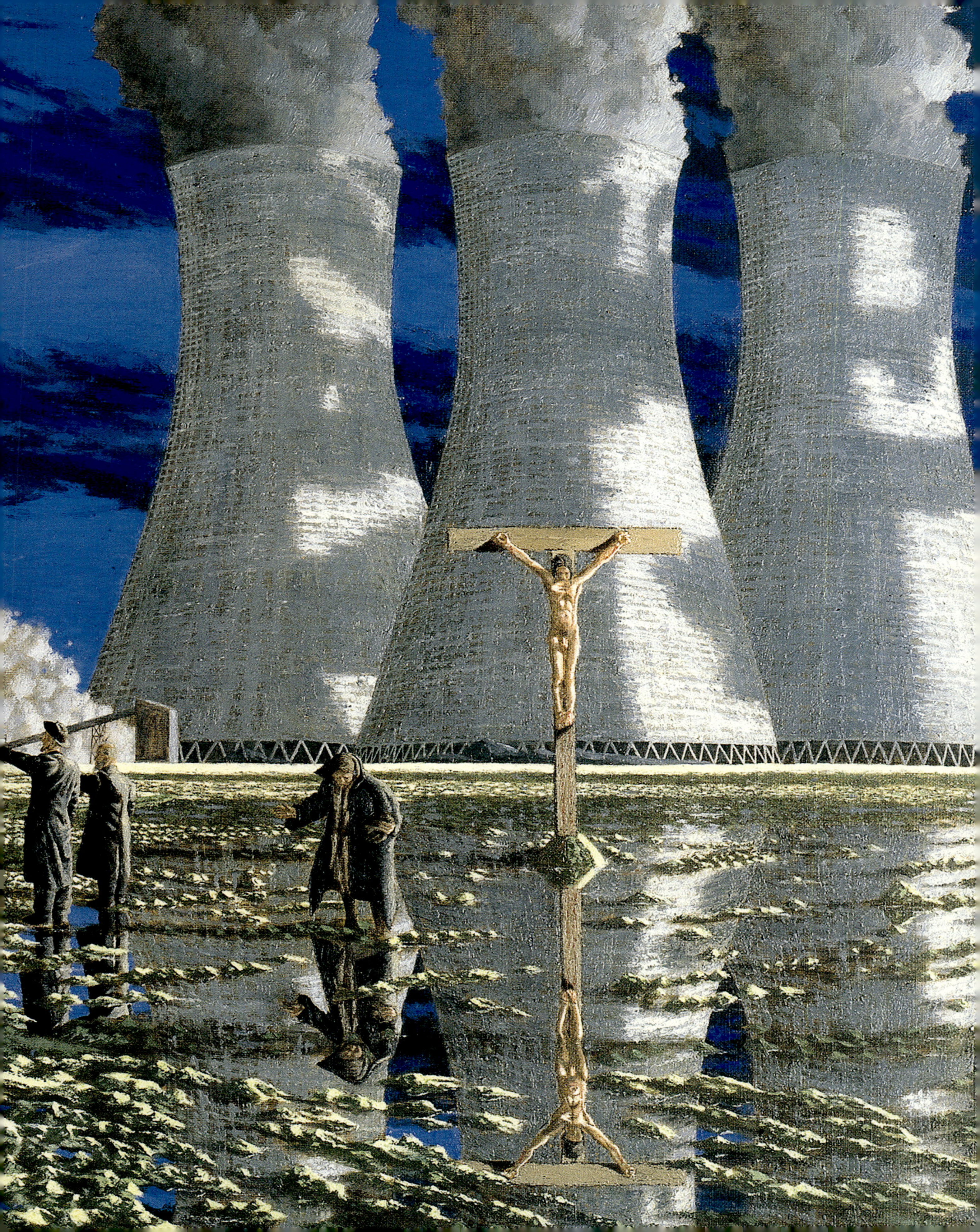

That Wagner's paintings constantly return to the motif of faith should not therefore surprise us. A gifted lay preacher, he contemplated abandoning his art for ordination, only to recognize the nature of his vocation. The fifteenth of the Fire Sonnets speaks of 'walking on water' as a metaphor of freedom in faith:

> That we in being loved might love again
> That overwhelming love that sets us free
> To step out of ourselves onto that sea.

It is no surprise, then, that *Walking on Water* is the title of several of Wagner's paintings, in the second of which Peter stretches out a hand across the glassy floor of a turbulent sea. In the third [p58], set before Battersea power station, the ragged figures of Christ and Peter reach out toward one another at flat low water. The painting rehearses Wagner's predilection for combining the vast symmetries of the industrial order with key moments in the histories of the two Testaments. The politics of transcendence is evident as never before. Here, at Battersea, it seems the situation is already more drastic, more desperate. The power of the vast buildings in the backdrop has long since departed. Peter is alone and ragged. He too will sink. He too will be rescued. But on his faith rather than the bricks and mortar of human power must Christ's kingdom rest.

Faith is indeed the bedrock of Wagner's painting. The expression of this faith places his work firmly in the long tradition of Christian art, whose task was never less than evangelical. To those for whom such an art is by nature imitative and reactionary, the reply is clear; these are new images, their symmetries and symbolic order gentle admonitions of the possibility of beauty, their complexity beyond the scope of abstraction in their semantic and symbolic wealth. They are a record of both the world Wagner has seen and of the role of faith in its construction. Wagner does not dwell on the infernal because for him the meaning of faith is the cosmic joy of which the Fire Sonnets speak. To write those words and make these images in a 'strangely' secular land has called for a courage more radical than that required to make the next 'gesture' in the endless unravelling of the twentieth-century avant-garde. I have watched Roger Wagner taking his successive steps onto the artistic waters over some thirty years with increasing admiration. He and his art have been borne up by the arms of faith.

Chris Miller was born in Iraq in 1955. He studied classics at Oxford and has worked in Paris, Copenhagen and Bogotá. He is a freelance translator, editor and critic, a longstanding contributor to *European Photography* and a contributing editor of *The Warwick Review*. A founder and director of the Oxford Amnesty Lectures, he has edited the OAL volumes *The Dissident Word* (1996) and *War on Terror* (forthcoming, MUP).

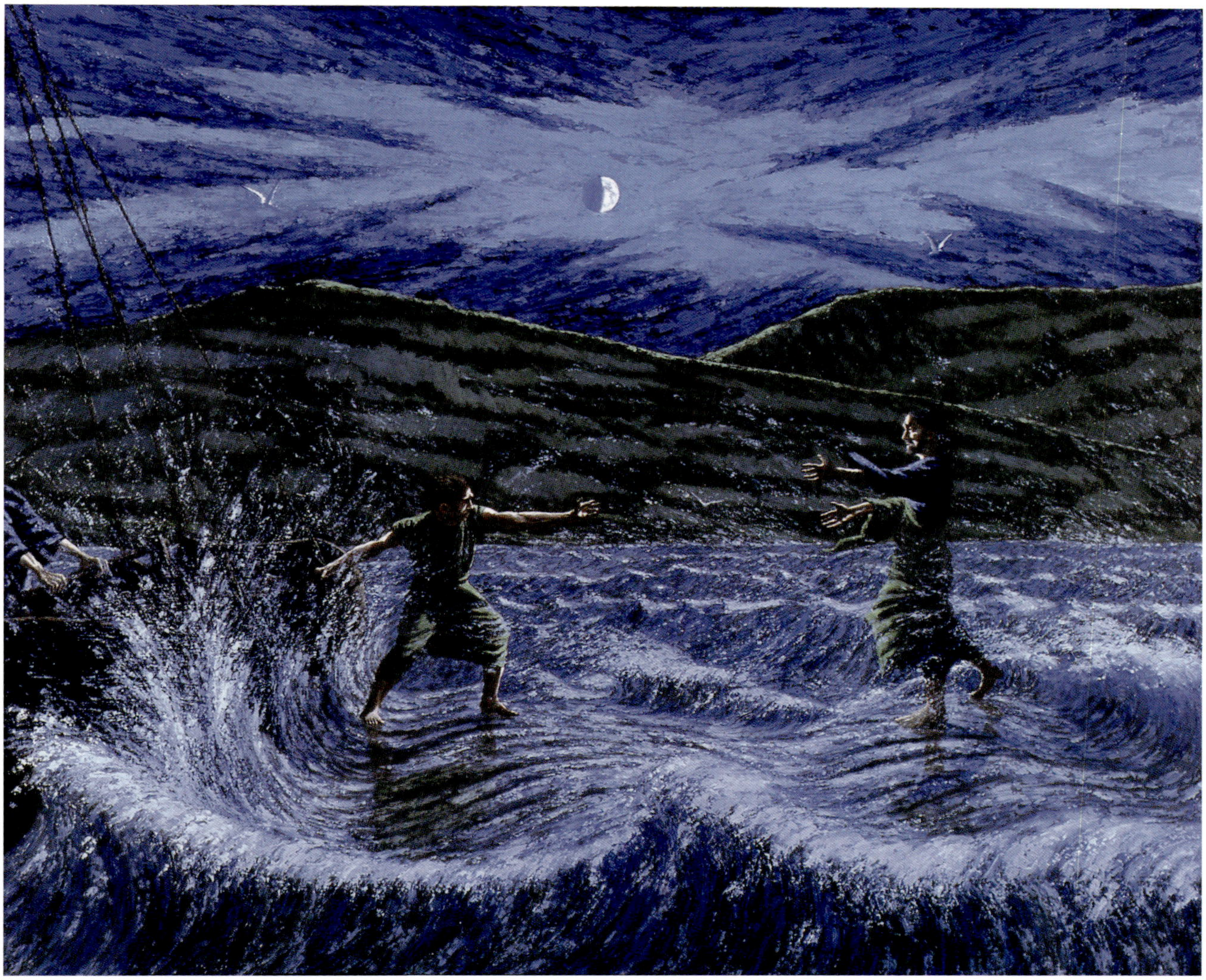

Walking on Water II (2005)

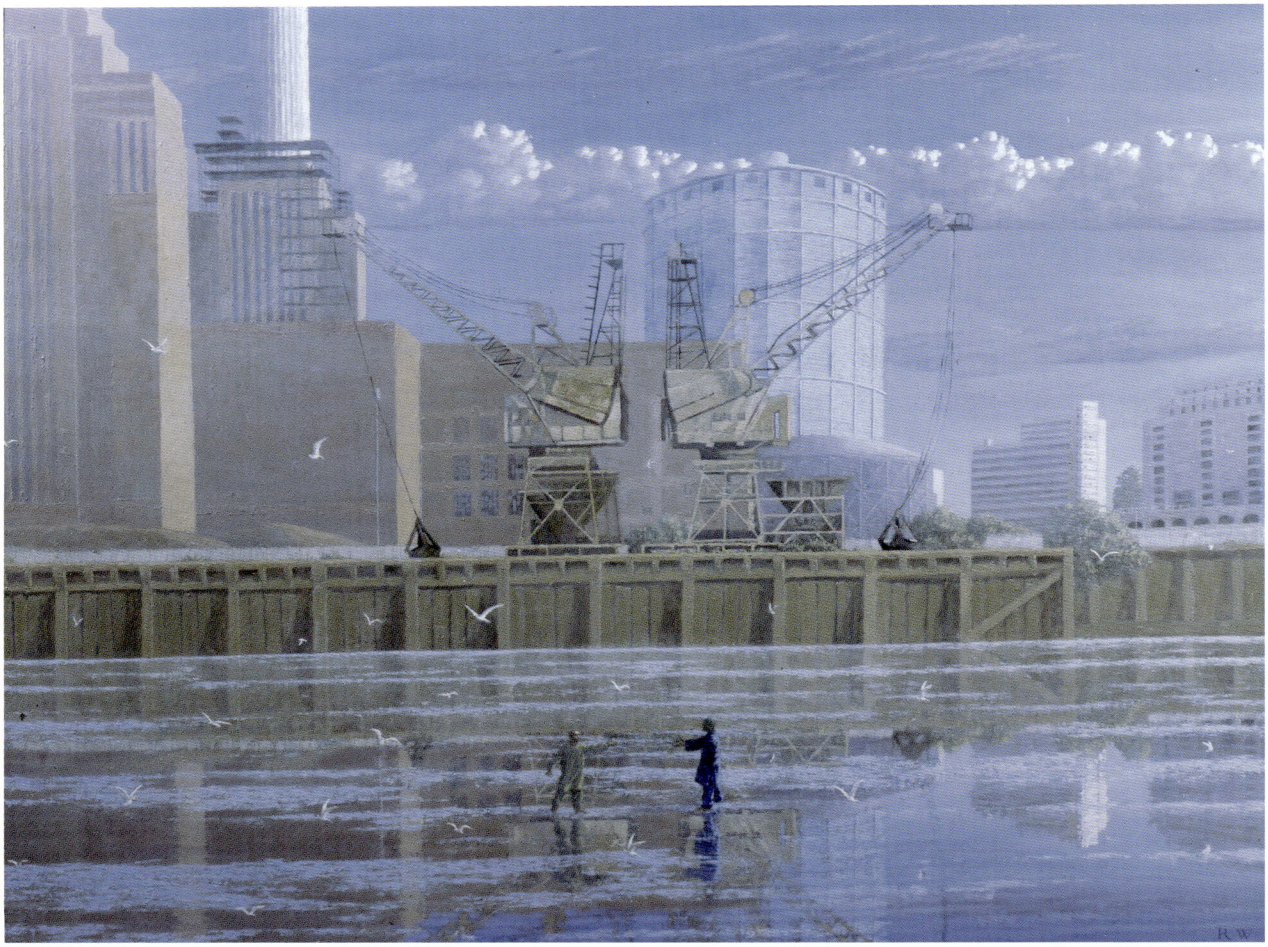

Walking on Water III (2005)

Roger Wagner

Born 1957

Academic

1975–78 Lincoln College, Oxford University: BA English Language and Literature
1978–81 Royal Academy School of Art

Individual Exhibitions

1985	Anthony Mould Contemporary, London
1986	Gallery 44, The Aldeburgh Festival
1988	Anthony Mould Contemporary, London
1994	The Ashmolean Museum, Oxford
1996	The Bartlemas Chapel, Oxford
1996	Anthony Mould Contemporary, London
1997	Ely Cathedral
1997	Norwich Cathedral
1997	Edmundsbury Cathedral
1997	Southwark Cathedral
1998	Wells Cathedral
1998	Chester Cathedral
1999	Anthony Mould Contemporary, London
2000	Anthony Mould Contemporary, London
2001	The Prince's Foundation, London
2001	Worcester Cathedral
2004	Lady Margaret Hall, Oxford University
2004	Anthony Mould Contemporary, London
2006	Phillip Mould Historical Portraits, London

Group Exhibitions

1981	Royal Academy Diploma show
1989–90	New Icons: Mead Gallery, University of Warwick; Royal Albert Museum, Exeter; Usher Gallery, Lincoln
1991	Images of Christ: Albemarle Gallery, London
1993	Images of Christ: Northampton Gallery and St Paul's Cathedral
1994	The NatWest Collection: The Royal Society of Arts
1995	The NatWest Collection: The Royal Academy
1999	Landscape and Imagination: The Prince of Wales Architecture Institute, London
1999–2000	The Light of the World: City Art Centre, Edinburgh
1999	Europe, Art et Passages: Mairie of the 9e Arrondissement, Paris
2000	The Salutation: St Andrew's Church, Oxford
2001	Help the Hospices Auction: Thomas Gibson Fine Art and Sothebys, both London
2001	Blake's Heaven: Scolar Fine Art, London
2002	Roads to Damascus: The Brewhouse Gallery, Eton College, Eton
2004	Presence: St Paul's Cathedral

2004 Loughborough University
2004 The North Light Gallery, Armitage Bridge, nr. Huddersfield
2004 The Ark-T Centre, Oxford
2005 St Giles Church, Oxford
2006 Queen's College, Oxford University
2007 Queen's College, Oxford University
2007 Blake's House, London University
2008 Exeter College, Oxford University

Collections

The Ashmolean Museum, Oxford
The Fitzwilliam Museum, Cambridge
The Natwest Collection, London
Eton College, Eton
Canary Wharf Ltd, London
The Takeover Panel, London
Lady Margaret Hall, Oxford University
The Vintners Company, London
Odey Asset Management, London

Bibliography

Writings by Roger Wagner

1984 *Fire Sonnets*. Oxford: The Besalel Press
1988 *In a Strange Land*. Oxford: The Besalel Press
1993 *Out of the Whirlwind*. Carlisle: Solway
1994 *The Book of Praises: A Translation of the Psalms (Book One)*. Oxford: The Besalel Press
1996 *A Silent Voice*. Oxford: The Besalel Press
2006 'Art and Faith', in *Public Life and the Place of the Church*. Farnham: Ashgate Publishing
2008 *The Book of Praises: A Translation of the Psalms* (Book Two). Oxford: The Besalel Press

Writings about Roger Wagner

1985 Peter Levi. *In a Strange Land,* exh. cat. Anthony Mould Ltd, London
1986 `Shoreham in Dockland'. *The Tablet,* 18 June
1989 Rupert Martin. *New Icons,* exh. cat. Mead Gallery, University of Warwick
1990 Pamela Tudor-Craig. 'Disturbing Glimpse…'. *The Church Times,* 16 February
1990 Jane Norrie. 'New Icons'. *Arts Review,* 23 February

1990 Cyril Barrett. 'Towards a New Iconography'. *Modern Painters* 3, no1
1993 Tom Devonshire Jones, ed. *Images of Christ,* exh. cat. St Matthew's Church, Northampton
1994 Chris Miller. *Roger Wagner Paintings 1982-1994,* exh. cat. Ashmolean Museum, Oxford
1994 Chris Miller. *'Seeing and Believing'. Oxford Today* 6, no2, Hilary
1994 Godfrey Barker. 'An English Visionary of Genius'. *The Daily Telegraph,* 31 January
1994 Giles Auty. 'A Need for Edens'. *The Spectator,* 5 February
1994 Paul Oldfield. 'Roger Wagner'. *The Oxford Times,* 28 January
1994 Sonia Khan. 'Apocalypse at the Ashmolean'. *The Word,* January
1994 Pamela Tudor-Craig. 'A Visionary Painter…'. *The Church Times,* 11 February
1994 Felix Martin. 'A New World Vision'. *The Word*
1995 Rupert Martin. 'Roger Wagner's Visionary Landscapes'. *Image Journal* 10
1995 Katherine Eustace. `Foreword', *Roger Wagner Paintings,* exh. cat. Anthony Mould Ltd, London
1995 Richard Davey. 'Christ the Teacher'. *The Church Times,* 3 November
1997 Sevie Riedinger. *Europe, Art et Passages,* exh. cat. Mairie du 9e, Paris
1998 David Patterson. *The Salutation,* exh. cat. St Andrews Church, Oxford
1998 David Thistlethwaite. *The Art of God and the Religions of Art.* Carlisle: Solway
1999 Alan Powers. *A Silent Voice,* exh. cat. Anthony Mould Ltd, London
1999 Helen de Borchgrave. *A Journey into Christian Art.* Oxford: Lion Publishing
1999 David Patterson, ed. *The Light of the World,* exh. cat. City Art Centre, Edinburgh
2001 Nicholas Cranfield. 'Blue Heaven'. *Church Times,* 1 June
2002 Daphne Facey. *Borderlands,* thesis. AUP, Cambridge.
2004 Rowan Williams. *Presence,* exh. cat. Bible Lands, High Wycombe
2004 Rowan Williams. 'Imitations of Christ'. *The Guardian,* 31 January
2004 Alan O'Sullivan. 'Past and Present Meet'. *The Baptist Times,* 18 November
2004 Richard Harries. *The Passion in Art.* Farnham: Ashgate Publishing
2004 Rupert Martin. *Seeing Salvation Now,* exh. cat. North Light Gallery, Armitage Bridge
2004 Margaret Barker. *An Extraordinary Gathering of Angels.* London: MQ Publications
2005 *Theology and the Power of the Spirit,* Grosvenor Essay 2
2005 Rowan Williams. 'Presence'. *Art and Christianity* 43, July
2005 Paula Clifford. `Angels…'. *Oxford Times,* September
2009 Theodore L. Prescott. 'Desire and Longing'. *Image Journal* 60

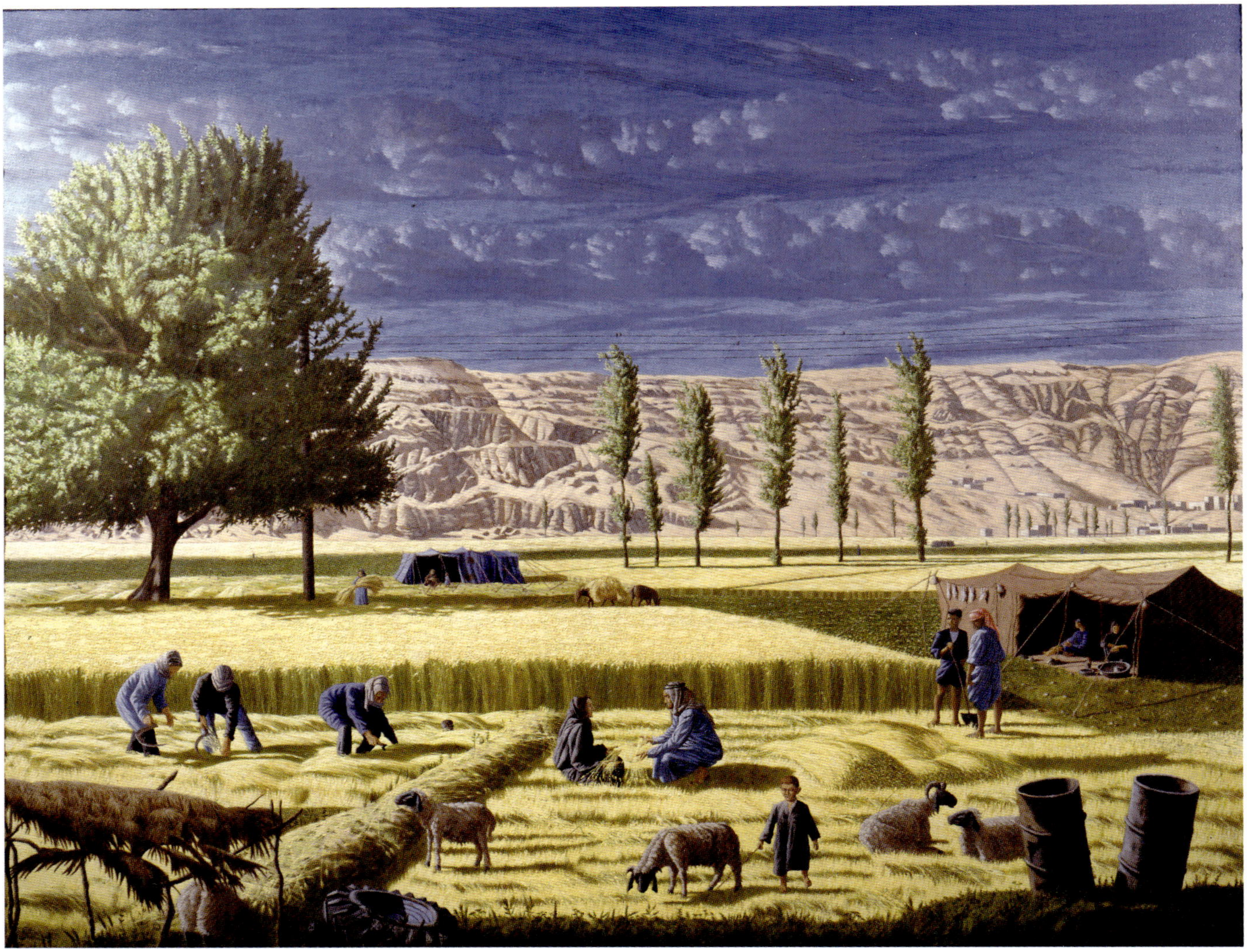

Ruth and Boaz (2000)

List of Images

Cover Front: *The Harvest Is the End of the World and the Reapers Are Angels* (1989), detail
Cover Back: *Menorah, study* (1993). Oil on board, 67 x 54.5 cm

VISIBILIA series, no. 4
This first edition, limited print run of 1000 copies

PO Box 83, Carlisle, CA3 9GR, UK
www.piquanteditions.com

British Library Cataloguing in Publication Data

Miller, Chris.
Forms of transcendence : the art of Roger Wagner. --
(Visibilia series ; no. 4)
1. Wagner, Roger. 2. Christian art and symbolism--Great
Britain.
I. Title II. Series III. Wagner, Roger.
759.2-dc22

ISBN-13: 9781903689554

PiQUANT editions

Design: Jonathan Kearney
Cover images: back, *The Harvest is the End of the World and the Reapers are Angels* (1989);
front, *Menorah, Study* (1993)